The Enneagram:

The Modern Guide To The 27 Sacred Personality Types – For Healthy Relationships In Couples And Finding The Road Back To Spirituality Within You

Beatrice Christian & Richard Stabile

© **Copyright 2019 - All rights reserved.**

The content contained within this book may not be reproduced, duplicated or transmitted without direct written permission from the author or the publisher.

Under no circumstances will any blame or legal responsibility be held against the publisher, or author, for any damages, reparation, or monetary loss due to the information contained within this book. Either directly or indirectly.

Legal Notice:

This book is copyright protected. This book is only for personal use. You can't amend, distribute, sell, use, quote or paraphrase any part, or the content within this book, without the consent of the author or publisher.

Disclaimer Notice:

Please note the information contained within this document is for educational and entertainment purposes only. All effort has been executed to present accurate, up to date, and reliable, complete information. No warranties of any kind are declared or implied. Readers acknowledge that the author isn't engaging in the rendering of legal, financial, medical or professional advice. The content within this book has been derived from various sources. Please consult a licensed professional before attempting any techniques outlined in this book.

By reading this document, the reader agrees that under no circumstances are is the author responsible for any losses, direct or indirect, which are incurred as a result of the use of information contained within this document, including, but not limited to, — errors, omissions, or inaccuracies.

Table of Contents

Table of Contents — 3

Introduction To Enneagram — 6

Chapter 01: Origins — 8
- *Why This Matters To You* — 11
- *What This Book Is About* — 12
- *The Dark Side Of Personality Tests* — 13

Section I Understanding The Basics And Background Of The System — 15

Chapter 02: The Theory of Enneagram — 16

Chapter 03: Understanding The Modern Day Enneagram of Personality Tool — 19

Chapter 04: Introduction To Enneagram Types — 22

Chapter 05: Structure Of The Diagram — 24
- *The centers:* — 27
- *The Wings:* — 31

SECTION II The Enneagram Personality Types In Detail — 34

Chapter 06: The Enneagram Of Personality Types — 35
- *Type One: The Perfectionist also called the Reformer* — 35
- *How to self-improve:* — 36
- *Your Wings* — 37
- *Type Two: The Giver also called the Helper* — 39
- *How to self-improve:* — 40
- *Your Wings* — 41
- *Type Three: The Achiever also called the Performer* — 43
- *How to self-improve:* — 44
- *Your Wings* — 46
- *Type Four: The Romantic also called the Individualist* — 48
- *How to self-improve:* — 49
- *Your Wings* — 50
- *Type Five: The Observer also called the Investigator* — 52
- *How to self-improve:* — 53

Your Wings	55
Type Six: The Doubter also called the Loyal skeptic	57
How to self-improve:	58
Your Wings	59
Type Seven: The Dreamer also called the Enthusiast	61
How to self-improve:	62
Your Wings	64
Type Eight: The Challenger also called the Leader	66
How to self-improve:	67
Your Wings	69
Type Nine: The Peacemaker also called the Diplomat	71
How to self-improve:	72
Your Wings	74

Section III: Instincts, Subtypes and variants within the Enneagram of Personality Tool — 76

Chapter 07: Diving Deeper into who you really are — 77

Self-preservation Instinct:	78
Social Instinct:	79
Sexual Instinct:	79
1. Personality Type One: The Perfectionist also called the Reformer	82
2. Personality Type Two: The Giver also called the Helper	84
3. The Achiever also called the Performer	87
4. The Romantic also called the Individualist.	90
5. The Observer also called the Investigator.	93
6. The Doubter also called the Loyalist.	96
7. The Dreamer also called the Enthusiast.	99
8. The Challenger also called the Leader.	102
9. The Peacemaker also called the Diplomat.	105
How to know your subtype:	108

Section IV: Using The Enneagram To Enrich Your Life — 112

Chapter 08: Integrating an ancient tool into a modern living — 113

Chapter 09: Accelerating your personal growth and self-expression — 115

Type One: The fear of being evil or corrupt.	117

Type Two: The fear of being unloved or unwanted by others 117
Type Three: The fear of being worthless and unaccomplished 118
Type Four: The fear of lacking a unique, special and significant identity. 118
Type Five: The fear of being helpless and inadequate. 119
Type Six: The fear of being without support or guidance. 119
Type Seven: The fear of deprivation and pain 120
Type Eight: The fear of being harmed or controlled by others 120
Type Nine: The fear of loss and separation from others. 121

Chapter 10: Enneagram Test   **123**
Type one: Reformer 123
Type Two: Helper 123
Type Three: Achiever 123
Type Four: Romantic 124
Type Five: Observer 124
Type six: Loyalist 125
Type seven: Enthusiast 125
Types eight: Challenger 125
Type nine: Peacemaker 126

Chapter 11: Cultivating Healthy Loving Relationships   **127**
When it comes to finding love and cultivating relationships: 132
Type One: The Reformer 132
Type Two: The Giver 132
Type Three: The Achiever 133
Type Four: The Romantic 133
Type Five: The Observer 134
Type Six: The Loyalist 134
Type seven: The Enthusiast 135
Type eight: The Challenger 135
Type nine: The Peacemaker 136

Chapter 12: Mapping out your path of most joy and fulfillment   **137**
How the Enneagram can help you grow and manifest a joy-filled life. 141

Introduction To Enneagram

Most of us go through life trying to deal with its struggles, challenges, and demands utterly unaware of the fact that there is a difference between the true self and the personality ego self that deals with everyday living. To "be yourself" is easier said than done in our society because we often get tangled up in mass consciousness and status quo leaving very little room for authentic self-expression and self-understanding. That's what the Enneagram is all about. It's a tool designed to help you simplify and increase your knowledge of self and in the process transcend your present level of human consciousness.

In a world layered with illusions, where everyone wears a mask on a daily basis, those who've grown tired of masquerades are thirsty for truth and authentic self-expression. This isn't something new; the quest has been ongoing for centuries now. Since the time of Socrates and even further back, there have always been those seeking the real knowledge of who they are. However, something is changing in our society.

Humanity is making a momentous leap in consciousness whereby as our lives become more complex, we experience the need to develop higher, better, more complex thinking and behaviors in order to cope. What most of us are discovering though is this approach isn't working too well.

The best way to thrive as the world continues to make a global shift isn't to seek more complicated coping mechanisms to tackle the new emerging world but rather, to simplify the way we relate to and partner up with life. In other words, we realize the better option is to seek simple solutions to our complex problems. We are learning to prioritize and appreciate this quest for truth and have become curious to discover if indeed there is more to us than what we've grown to believe about ourselves.

   Have you reached a point in your life where the need to discover who you really as has increased yet you don't know where to start? Sometimes it can be tough understanding your own behavior and actions or why you react the way you do in certain situations. It's a very sobering moment when you wake up one day to the realization that you don't even know who you really are - deep inside. The pathway to the inner world is filled with great mystery and can often intimidate us especially when we've been locked out of our own truth for decades. That's where tools and proven systems become useful.

   Enneagram is an ancient system and tool that was created to help those of us who care about uncovering the layers of mass consciousness so we can dive deep to discover our true self. And this book is designed to help make that journey of self-discovery and this ancient tool more straightforward, understandable, and quick to utilize.

Chapter 01: Origins

The term Enneagram is of Greek origins. Ennea is the number nine in Greek, and gram means a drawing. Translated into ordinary English, we would interpret it as a drawing with nine points.

In section one of this book, we will explore in great detail what this drawing looks like and means. For now, the critical thing to realize is that we're not just talking about some new age methodology cooked up to help you cope with the increasing stresses of life. There's more to it than meets the eye.

At first, it may just appear to be another one of those entertaining yet juvenile personality tests that don't possess any concrete basis to assure personal transformation, but if you read through the context of this material and apply right understanding to it, you'll reap the benefits of the power contained.

The earliest version of this concept is said to have been developed around the 4th century by a Christian mystic, Evagrius Ponticus who identified eight deadly thoughts plus an overarching thought he called "self-love." In addition to identifying eight deadly thoughts, Evagrius also identified "remedies" to these thoughts. (Enneagram of Personality From Wikipedia, the free encyclopedia)

Some present-day teachers of this material believe that variations of the Enneagram symbol can be traced to the sacred geometry of Pythagorean mathematicians and mystical mathematicians. Although there is much dispute over this theory and who actually originated it, the fact of the matter is that it works and is being widely used in both the business world and for spiritual growth. While the Enneagram symbol itself does have its roots in antiquity, many individuals in various ways developed the actual system that we use today not too long ago.

George Gurdijieff, a Russian mystic, and teacher is one such individual who is credited with the modern reintroduction of the Enneagram symbol. He was a founder of a highly influential school specializing in 'inner work' and his primary way of teaching and using the symbol was through a series of sacred dances or what he called 'movements.' He believed in giving his students a direct sense of the meaning of the symbol and the process it represents but what he did not do was include the system of ennea-types, as we know it today. For us to understand who was behind this system, as we know it today, we'll have to introduce Oscar Ichazo into the story.

Oscar Ichazo is credited as the primary individual behind the contemporary Enneagram system. He was a Bolivian man who moved to Peru and later to Buenos Aries in Argentina to study 'inner work.' This led to further travel and wisdom-seeking in Asia where he gathered more knowledge across various wisdom traditions which helped him create a systematic way of understanding and applying all he had learned in his voyages. Ichazo combined teachings from Taoism, Buddhism, ancient Greek philosophy, Islam, Christianity, and mystical Judaism to form his own school of thought that utilized the use of the ancient Enneagram symbol. Thus from the 1960s when he started his teachings in Chile, the personality-based Enneagram was offered as a system to help with self-realization and transformation.

The Arica school in Chile where he taught in the 1960s and early 1970s is where he first introduced his system of 108 Enneagrams (or Ennneagons, in his terminology) but the Enneagram movement in America has been based on the first few, primarily on four of them. These are called the Enneagram of the

Passions, the Enneagram of the Virtues, the Enneagram of the Fixations, and the Enneagram of the Holy Ideas. (The Traditional Enneagram, enneagraminstitute.com)

It was during this time in Chile that an American group interested in his work came to South America to study and experience firsthand his methods. One of the participants in the group was notable American psychologist Claudio Naranjo who went on to recreate his updated version of the Enneagram personality system. Although Ichazo and Naranjo started off as teacher and student, they've each gone their separate ways teaching different theories of this Enneagram system and seeing as there continue to be different schools of thought emerging on the subject, don't be surprised to find that some ideas do not always align. The fundamental objective, however, isn't to get into a debate over who is right or wrong. We are here to develop a healthy way of understanding and relating to our human psyche. This tool has proven very useful for those who practice with diligence, and it will help you better understand the people around you and yourself.

Why This Matters To You

Understanding why you behave as you do and finding a healthy way to bring out the hidden powers, talents, and aspects of you that would otherwise remain dormant can increase your personal happiness and those of your loved ones.

It's also an empathy enhancer. The more you understand why people behave as they do, the less likely you are to take things personally, get thrown off your own alignment or even misunderstand them. Now that we've become more connected than ever as a global community, there's a greater need for compassion, understanding, and empathy. At work, on social media, in public gatherings, and at home. It helps when human behavior isn't such a mystery to you because you can intelligently assess any given situation and respond rather than react when you have a bearing of the main underlying motives driving human consciousness.

Bottom line is this.

Anything we can do to know more about ourselves and become better humans is worth diving into and investing a little effort. It takes an open mind and heart, but if you're ready to soak in some new healthy perspectives, I promise to deliver the insights that can aid you.

What This Book Is About

Simply put, this book will answer the big question. Why do you do what you do whether or not it's voluntary? It unveils the underlying motives behind each of us, and it will help you gain clarity on the patterns that are not serving you so you can improve upon them as well as shine a light on the positive traits that you need to be taking advantage of.

You will finally discover the real you and become empowered enough to discern the difference between the mask you've been wearing as a form of protection all your life and the real authentic self that is you. Not only will you learn more about yourself, but you'll also begin to see the world with fresh new eyes understanding why people think, feel, behave and act as they do. This will enable you to spot those that you are most compatible with and nurture more of those relationships. In fact, I have a chapter that explicitly aids you in cultivating healthy loving relationships.

I commend you on making this choice to improve yourself and better understand your fellow human beings. Your personal success and happiness will be directly impacted by the changes and practices that you integrate as you absorb each chapter.

The book is divided into four sections. In section one, we get back to basics so you can form a solid foundation before integrating this into your life and relationships. In section two, we'll dive into the details of the Enneagram types. In section three we explore more of who you really are as well as the subtypes of the Ennea -types and lastly, I will practically walk you through integrating this into the areas of your life that matter the most. You'll also have the chance to do an Enneagram test to find out which type and subtypes most resonate with you. Now, remember, Enneagram system is a work in progress as is your life. Be easy with yourself as you go through this process and try not to get too rigid trying to fit into one specific type or subtype.

The Dark Side Of Personality Tests

A woman was performing incredibly well at her job leading a small team in a major real estate agency until she took one of the more commonly praised personality tests. After receiving the personality test results, her colleagues didn't trust her the same way. They felt she just didn't have the right personality to be in that position.

In sharing her frustration with me, she said: " after that day, anytime something goes wrong, or I make a mistake I just have this unshakeable feeling that it's because I'm this particular personality type and perhaps I should be looking for work that's better suited to that type of personality." She's worried all her colleagues also feel the same way and it creates tension that just wasn't there before in her leadership abilities. This is a real and common problem that a lot of people report once they fall into the downside of continually relying on shallow personality tests.

The mistake here is elementary. When we apply rigid labels to ourselves and others that limit the ability to do things that fall outside those test results it can be like being locked in a tiny box. I want you to avoid that erred thinking as we jump into the basics of the Enneagram system. In order for you to use this tool effectively, you must understand a very simple fact.

You are a dynamic ever-evolving human being. Your experiences, environment, and state of mind regularly change, and so does your personality type. This nine-point system isn't meant to box you into one category. All nine points are interconnected, and you may find aspects of you in several types. This is a good thing.

Being able to discover more of who you really are is possible and can be done without necessarily fitting into one rigid category. Let's get started.

Section I
Understanding The Basics And Background Of The System

Chapter 02: The Theory of Enneagram

If we truly want a better understanding of the Enneagram and how it's meant to help us lead better lives, we must at the very least take to account the primary purpose of Ichazo's work.

We have to distinguish between a man as he is in essence and as he is in ego or personality. In reality, every person is perfect, fearless and in loving unity with the entire cosmos; there is no conflict within the person between head, heart, and stomach or between the person and others.

Then something happens: the ego begins to develop, karma accumulates, there is a transition from subjectivity to objectivity; man falls from essence into personality (Interviews with Ichazo, page 9)

The actual theory of the Enneagram of personality types that he created is more than just offering you a quick test to help you fit into a specific category. It's about enlightening and prompting you to awaken to a better understanding of the structure of your soul as well as others. There is a real self and an everyday self that together form the individual you know yourself to be. Usually, we operate our entire lives from the ordinary self (also known as the ego-self) that we become estranged from that deep true self and that's where all the inner restlessness, confusion and identity crisis emerges from.

Ichazo developed his transformational teachings and methodologies to help us reconcile these two aspects of ourselves and bring back the harmony and wholeness that is our true nature.

So the enneagram is meant to equip you with a tool that helps you gain insight into your soul qualities and true essence, which Ichazo proposes to be distorted or contracted into states of ego. The theory is inspired by the western mystical and philosophical tradition of nine divine forms as discussed by Plato (platonic solids) and then further developed in the third century by the Neo-Platonic philosopher Plotinus in his work - The Enneads.

Clearly, these are far from new ideas but what we can conclude is no one had brilliantly consolidated all these different schools of thought in aiding self-awareness the way Ichazo did. The basis of his teaching is that as long as an individual is abiding in pure essence, they are in complete harmony with all of life and possess the higher essential qualities also known as the Holy Ideas.

Each Holy Idea has a corresponding Virtue. As an individual loses awareness and presence, they fall away from that pure Essence and enter the realm of personality where both the Holy Ideas and the Virtues become distorted into Ego-fixation and passion respectively.

Holy Ideas, Virtues, Ego-fixations, and Passions
According to Ichazo's theory, the loss of self-awareness leads to spiritual contraction, which gives way to ego states causing us to lose our groundedness and center. We become distorted in our thoughts, feelings, and actions disabling the connection with the Divine. He's not saying we're not supposed to have passions and ego-fixations but merely pointing out that these are lower untamed aspects of ourselves that are actually part of something bigger and better if we only learn to utilize

them effectively. Once we recognize they are distorted versions of the pure Essence, it becomes our quest to restore that balance and truth in our lives. This is the primary purpose underlying the Enneagram of personality.

The objective isn't just taking a test; it's what happens to you once you take that first step of self-analysis through the test.

Chapter 03: Understanding The Modern Day Enneagram of Personality Tool

Now that you have context on the purpose and origin of both the ancient Enneagram symbol as well as the concept created by Ichazo that includes the symbol that forms the Enneagram of personality, as we know it today let's shift our focus. It's time to take our attention from the basic history to the actual system so you can start seeing the value it can bring to the development of your life.

When attempting to understand and study human behavior, there are various approaches one can use. Most of them involve diagnosing pathological behaviors, and while this is important, it's certainly not a very holistic approach and does not consider human behavior in its entirety.

What the Enneagram is meant to do is offer a more holistic roadmap and a precise language to help you understand and express what you discover about yourself and others.

Although it is still unclear where the line can be drawn between Ichazo's work and Naranjo's further advancement of the system, a personal confirmation during an interview where Naranjo proclaimed that he took the work Ichazo had done to the next level by placing specific identities on the nine personality types leads me to conclude that Naranjo may be accredited to the detailed "type names" we'll be diving into in the section where we dissect each Enneagram type.

Regardless of the creator of the nine-point system, we know the twenty-first-century enneagram has evolved over the years. The detailed typing system needed to grow and factor in the psychological discoveries we've made in the modern world if it was to remain relevant.

It is our job to remember that the purpose of this tool isn't to label and categorize others or ourselves into certain fixed states. Instead, it's about opening you up to recognize the main behavioral patterns people tend to fall into, understanding that each individual can exhibit any one of these personality traits more dominantly than the other characteristics depending on their present state of being, environment and how self-aware they are.

In the interview where Claudio Naranjo explained better his role in the creation of the Enneagram of personality, as we know it today, he openly shares "When people say, "A [type] One is like this" or "a [type] Two is like that" or 'the pride type has such-and-such traits,' that comes from my own work. And that's why only people that came through my school became teachers of the Enneagram."

He goes on to say that what Ichazo had was a basic map that he helped develop to the advanced level we know it today. "I had cultivated the seed, and everything that emerged from my work was of that sort: fleshing in the skeletal information or the schemes he passed on." (Seeker After Truth: An Interview With Claudio Naranjo by Iain McNay. Watkins Magazine, 2016, October 14th)

To better understand the Enneagram of personality tool, we need to consider how the mind works. The mind wants to be strategic about handling and navigating life so you can best survive whatever comes your way. The nine-pointed system of the enneagram is said to be the nine distinct and unique qualities that all human beings possess as special characteristics to help an individual navigate life (including trauma).

Your Enneagram type is the navigational tool that's with you all the time secretly influencing your behavior, perceptions, and reactions in ways you may not always predict. The more you can understand your enneagram type the greater insight you'll have about yourself and your habitual patterns of thought because you'll recognize there's one primary way that you perceive and react to things demonstrating your dominant enneagram personality. This will enable you to make an informed decision on whether or not you would like to activate other characters that you feel are better suited to the kind of individual you aspire to be.

It will also help you better discern between the real self and the ego-self in you. It's a subtle yet complex system, but it doesn't need to overwhelm or confuse you. As we hit the core of this book and uncover this nine-pointed system, take a moment to pause in between the type description to see which ones resonate with you. Toward the end of the book, we'll do a simple enneagram test to help you figure out where you stand and which type is most dominant in your personality. But for now, let's explore each numbered point and the enneagram structure in greater detail.

Chapter 04: Introduction To Enneagram Types

Based on the teachings of the Enneagram of personality system, we know there are nine points. Each with a unique type name given.

1. The Perfectionist also called the Reformer.
2. The Giver also called the Helper.
3. The Achiever also called the Performer.
4. The Romantic also called the Individualist.
5. The Observer also called the Investigator.
6. The Loyalist also called the Doubter.
7. The Enthusiast also called the Dreamer.
8. The Challenger also called the Leader.
9. The Peacemaker also called the Diplomat.

It's worth mentioning however that there are more than just these nine types contained within the system. There are also centers and wings that play a significant role in the interpretation and understanding of your results when you do take the test.

The Centers:

The centers further arrange the nine points into three groupings. They form a triad on the diagram. Classifying the numbered points as the Instinctive center for type 1, 8 and 9; the Feeling center for type 2, 3 and 4; and finally the Thinking center for personality type 5, 6 and 7.

The Wings:

The wings are what help us recognize the fact that we are all connected regardless of type and we are also not exclusively and rigidly stuck to one numbered point. As a matter of fact, unless we embrace and develop "our wings" it's still going to be tough reaching our full potential in life.

We dive more into the centers and wings in the next chapter where you can even get a visual sense of the Enneagram to better help you connect with the system.

As you can see, there are added layers of complexities, which can be very intriguing to an individual who has an opening mind and seeks more profound truths. As complicated as this system may appear, it is very dynamic and rather simple once you understand and connect to the diagram structure itself because it will give your mind a working mental image from which to grasp more about your natural proclivities.

When trying to discover more about yourself, others and the reason why you behave as you do, the Internet does have lots of solutions to choose from. Unfortunately, most of them don't carry enough merit to give you an answer that can actually transform your entire life. The Enneagram personality tool, however, is one of the few globally recognized systems that not only helps you learn more about your personality, it also expands your awareness to show you ways you can tap into realms that go far beyond superficial trends. Best of all, it gives you insights on how your personality type will behave when exposed to unhealthy, stressful situations as well as how good things can be once you get on the healthy path of personality development.

Chapter 05: Structure Of The Diagram

The structure of the conventional Enneagram diagram is intended to help you visually, mentally and emotionally connect with the tool, showing you how the interrelation among the personality types works. Before we start dissecting it, I bet you're wondering why the system is numerically numbered 1-9. I was curious about it too. Does a higher numerical ranking imply that one personality type possesses more value?

Not at all! There's no difference in value between the larger and the smaller number. So just because someone is an eight does not signify they are better than a three.

I firmly believe that no type is better or worse than the other. Each character is unique with different attributes that can be expressed in healthy or unhealthy ways. Sure, you'll find some people desiring a specific number because according to society it's better to be that personality type, but I just don't agree with that notion. I think any symbol can become a handicap if underdeveloped. The key is to nurture the healthy aspects of whichever type you most resonate with. Don't fuss so much about what "people say" is the best personality. The best character for you is authentically being yourself and showing up as the highest version you can be.

The quickest way to understand the diagram is by starting from the outside layers and working your way in. Imagine drawing a circle. Then a triangle within the circle and let it touch all three corners. Mark the three points of the triangle 9, 3 and 6 in clockwise position with 9 sitting at the top of the circle.

All you have to do now is make six equidistant points from the circumference of the circle and designate the remaining numbers 1,2,4,5,7,8 to fill in the gaps. Be sure to do it symmetrically and in a clockwise motion. Each of these numbers represents one of the primary nine personality types. If you're doing this activity by hand, you will begin to notice that the nine points can be connected in some way by inner lines and that points 3, 6 and 9 actually form an equilateral triangle. The remaining six points can be connected as shown in the diagram below. The importance of these inner lines leads us to another vital lesson when it comes to an understanding of the Enneagram of personality tool.

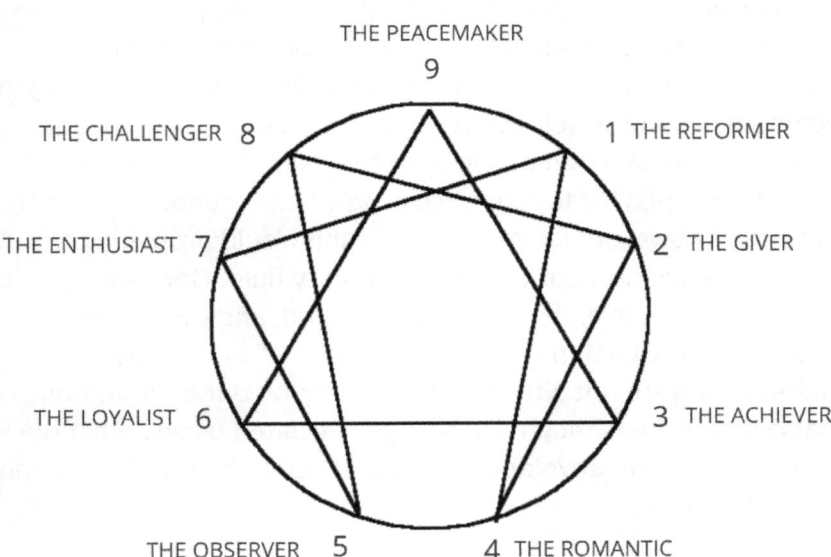

At a fundamental level, the tool is used to help a person identify their most dominant type within the nine-point system. However, there's more to it than meets the eye for those who want to dive deeper. There's also interconnectedness between the nine points. So while you may find your basic personality to be a 2, it isn't uncommon to discover a little more of yourself in all nine types. This is where the Centers and Wings come into play.

All teachers and authors of Enneagram agree that we are all born with a particular dominant personality type, which emerges in childhood to help us adapt to our environment.

As infants, we don't really have a developed sense of self. The ego has not yet been activated and if you're unclear about this just spend some time in a park. Notice how the tiny infant in a pram has no sense of identity. He or she can barely tell the difference between their toes and fingers or whether a doll belongs to them or not. Then observe toddlers who are starting to become more a little self-aware. They can identify their parents and siblings but still don't have a sense of self. Then we have the five-year-olds playing together, chasing a ball around. The owner of the ball knows it belongs to her and she would probably cry if you grab it from her, but the self is still very fluid. Once they get to age seven and above, the self is well defined, and everything is about taking ownership and determining "me" and "mine." As children, we were not different. Depending on our environment, what our caregivers taught us, how they treated us and what we got exposed to, we developed a sense of self to help us fit into this world and survive.

We may, therefore, generalize that our formative years and all we were exposed to help shape our personalities. We learned to depend more heavily on the personality type that would enable us to survive and feel safe in the world around us. Some of what we ended up choosing may be wonderful, but perhaps some aspects are not healthy at all yet we still show up in the world as that person. Furthermore, it might be that we've neglected to develop and leverage the influences of the connected qualities and special abilities we may possess. That's why getting to know what center you belong to and what wings you're in possession of can be worthwhile. Let us further discuss the role of the three centers and the wings before jumping into each of the nine points on the next section.

The centers:

As mentioned earlier, Centers are segmented into a triad. These are centers of intelligence into which each of the numbered points will fall. Each center will contain three personality types. The triad consists of the thinking center, the feeling center, and the gut center.

Also known as the head, heart and gut centers respectively. These centers are designed and designated to the specific areas on the diagram intentionally. The centers are usually differentiated from each other based on how the person usually interprets life and others.

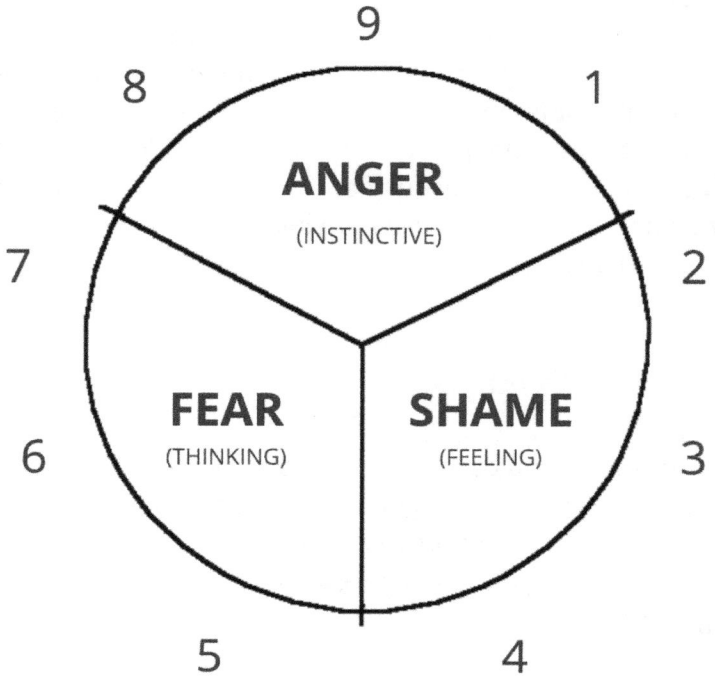

The Thinking Center:

The head types are usually too stuck in their head. They tend to withdraw from relationships. The head center is a cognitive center and the people in this triad love to think, analyze, and approach things with caution. Picture for a moment that you were at a party. If you're part of the thinking center, then your natural tendency and preference would be standing at or close to the door so you can have a better view and merely observe others.

Some authors like to refer to them as mental based types. Their dominant emotion to keep in check is Fear.

The Feeling Center:

The heart types are usually people who engage in relationships and continuously seek out others. They are very concerned with feelings and their interactions with other people. Go back to that party scene again. This time instead of standing by the door to see who is present and what's happening around you, you'd be the first to mingle, introduce yourself to people and try to connect with as many people as possible.

Some authors will refer to these types as feeling-based types. Their dominant emotion to keep in check is Shame.

The Instinctive Center:

The gut types are instinctual. They are very direct and aren't afraid to be confrontational. People in this triad tend to act first and think and feel later. If we take that party example one last time, you'd know if this triad if your perfect fit by your approach from the moment you entered the room. Are you bold, loud, hearty and jovial in your interaction with others? Perhaps you come off too strong which others often find offensive or intimidating. And if your the type of person that isn't shy when it comes to offering constructive criticism even if it is to the host of the party, then I'd say, this is your center of intelligence.

Some authors will refer to these types as body based types. The dominant emotion to keep in check here is Anger.

According to the Enneagram Institute, each type results from a particular relationship with a cluster of issues that characterize that center. Most simply, these issues revolve around a powerful, mostly unconscious emotional response to the loss of contact with the core of the self. (How the Enneagram system works via The Enneagram Institute)

So in other words, you have a specific unconscious emotional response that often surfaces as a result of the loss of contact between the everyday little self and the true self. The three centers having been grouped into Thinking, Instinctive and Feeling centers have as their dominant emotions Fear, Anger, and Shame respectively.

So if you take the Enneagram test and discover you're a type 6 and after a little reflection it dawns on you that fear is definitely one of the biggest paralyzers holding you back from greatness, then you've just confirmed that you're dominantly in the Thinking Center.

The more disconnected you are from your true self; the tighter the grip of fear will be because that's the dominant unconscious emotion. So when you're improving your life and working hard to manifest a life you love, it's important to keep a close watch on fear because that would be your biggest sabotager.

Each center of intelligence has certain liabilities and assets that are included in it which the assigned personality types that come under that group will possess. For example, type three falls into the "feeling center." This suggests their most dominant unconscious emotion to watch out for is shame. It also means there are certain strengths and qualities they would possess in relation to "feelings" which is why they fall into that triad.

Just so we're clear, this doesn't mean you won't experience other emotions. Think of the group you're in as containing a theme. Whatever your theme is, that will be your most dominant emotion to deal with.

The Wings:

The reason I believe wings are a significant aspect to include in your interpretation of your Enneagram results is that in truth, none of us can be entirely summed up by a single personality type.

We are unique and complex individuals. Ever evolving and changing from one moment to the next. Which means our character must also be a combination of various qualities. The wings help to integrate this concept into the system.

Although some teachers of the Enneagram argue that we only have one wing, I am convinced we must have more than one. Even if we judge it from a strictly numerical point of view, the number 1 is connected to 2 on one side and 9 on the other. The type adjacent to the 1 is what we refer to as your wing. Just as a bird or plane needs both wings to fly, you need wings to soar. These wings are supposed to compliment your core personality. They connect you to your "closest neighbors" giving you access to different resources and characteristics that can be quite useful.

Are both wings equally dominant and do you need to develop each one individually?

Yes and No. It's actually not an easy question to answer. The Enneagram Institute provides a little insight into this. "Observation of people leads us to conclude that while the two-wing theory applies to some individuals, most people have a dominant one. In the vast majority of people, while the so-called second wing always remains operative to some degree, the dominant wing is far more important."

I think the most important thing to recall when it comes to your wings is that you will resonate more with one side and that's okay. As years go by, that might change too, and you may find yourself switching and exhibiting more qualities of the wing that's less influential. Either way, it's good to become aware of both and figure out which one aligns best with your basic personality and the human being you want to become.

An effective way of approaching and understanding your wings:

Not too long ago I walked into my favorite frozen yogurt parlor to take a break from the hour-long mall shopping I had just finished. Unfortunately, I wasn't the only one in need of this refreshing break. It would be around 5 minutes waiting in line before I finally got my turn. Rather than scowl and feel sorry for myself I decided to observe what the people in front of me were ordering with their Yoghurt Ice-cream. It was a rather exciting experience when I realized how unique we all are. Some people wanted just the plain base with no toppings at all. Others wanted four different toppings.

A teenage girl just in front of me wanted to know if she could get six different toppings! I thought that was a little too much. By the time it was my turn, I felt quite modest when I asked for a medium sized frozen yogurt with just Nutella as the topping! Yes, I'm a Nutella junkie, what can I say?

Point of the story is this.

Just as we are all uniquely different with our topping preferences, the relationships with our wings will also vary from individual to individual. The wings are not the frozen yogurt; they are the toppings, which you can choose to flavor your frozen yogurt (core personality type) with. We all have access to both our wings, and at times one will be more predominant than the other.

The more you know your preference, the easier it becomes to use your wings. Some people don't like any topping at all. In this case, we would refer to them as a light wing; some want lots of toppings or too much of one kind. Those we might refer to as strong wing/s. Others like me want to have just the right amount of toppings, and we can refer to that as balanced double wings. Regardless of your preference, connecting to your wings can help you understand the subtleties of your core personality type.

As you lean more into your wings to one side or the other, you will expand your perspective and increase your capacity to deal with tension creating a bigger potential to reframe influencers that no longer serve you. Each core personality type comes with a connected "close neighbor" on each side of the nine-point system. Some of the gifts and challenges carried by each wing will be explored in the next section as we unlock the qualities of the core personality types. Let's get to it.

SECTION II The Enneagram Personality Types In Detail

Chapter 06: The Enneagram Of Personality Types

Type One: The Perfectionist also called the Reformer

A person in this category is usually considered a perfectionist. He or she enjoys feeling in control and has a constant need to do what's right. Some of the core values for a type one are integrity and responsibility.

Being considered a good person is critical to those who fall into this first type, often taking a more black and white approach to everything. Something is good or bad; wrong or right - it's just that simple for them. They are more body-based and are usually more attentive to the external than the internal world.

Famous celebrities such as Hilary Clinton, Martha Stewart or even world reformers like Nelson Mandela would probably fall into this type.

Certain qualities are attributed to the typical ones. Character traits such as purposeful, principled, self-controlled full of integrity and pragmatic.

They can be quite calm and serene, but they are also known to be very critical of themselves and others. They tend to be very uncompromising and judgmental. Since they fall into the

Instinctive Center, rage and anger are common experiences, but they do a good job suppressing it because they don't like to express emotions very much.

If you are a type one person, then you're more likely to be interested in doing the right thing at all times. Common sense is what you believe in, and you're very responsible often wondering what's wrong with people who don't take life seriously and own up to their responsibilities. You have high standards and tend to be an idealist doing the best you can to improve the world around you hence the common term "reformer." You're detail-oriented, precise in your manner of communication and grounded.

How to self-improve:

The best way to aid your personal growth if you resonate most with type one is to practice being less critical of yourself. Learn to release anger, rage, resentment or whatever else shows up healthily.

Learning to forgive yourself and others for mistakes will also be a liberating experience, as it will better empower you to deal with the imperfections that you become conscious of. Also, give yourself permission to have fun!

Your Wings

The Nine Wing:

Gifts:
Some of the gifts this wing brings to the strict perfectionist include but aren't limited to the following.

- That strong urge you often have to correct or improve people and things is significantly reduced.

- You are able to hold more viewpoints and be more open and collaborative.

There's an increased sense of relaxation, trust, and acceptance of others as they are.

Challenges:
Some of the challenges this wing has for the strict perfectionist include but aren't limited to the following.

- You may be less focused on tending to your personal needs and instead pour all your efforts on the needs of others, which could lead down an unhealthy path of self-neglect.

- The laid-back approach my turn unhealthy for you causing you to start procrastinating and neglecting important tasks.

The Two Wing:
Gifts:
Some of the gifts this wing brings to the strict perfectionist include but aren't limited to the following.

- You may notice your often critical attitude toward yourself and others is softened by compassion, empathy, and understanding.

- Idealism in you will be more easily expressed constructively in service to others.

Challenges:
Some of the challenges this wing brings to the strict perfectionist include but aren't limited to the following.

- You might have an increased desire to improve people and conditions just so you can feel accepted and worthwhile.

- There's a tendency to feel victimized or taken advantage of even as you sacrifice your own needs.

Type Two: The Giver also called the Helper

This type of person is naturally very empathic, caring and helpful to others hence the term "helper."

Think of an iconic figure like Diana - Princess of Wales or Mother Teresa and you've got a good grasp of this personality type. If we dared go too far, we could even assign religious archetypes such as Jesus Christ this numbered point.

Certain qualities are attributed to the type twos. Character traits such as authenticity, compassion, generosity, possessive and caring.
Because they have such a strong need for love, they can often become people pleasers.

A type two values relationships a lot and puts a lot of energy into them to the point where he or she may neglect his or her personal needs. Empaths would undoubtedly be considered to fall into this category mostly. Being a feeling-based type, they are grouped as part of the Feeling Center, and unfortunately, this leads to the dominant sense of shame.

Often, a person in this category will try to mask the shame they are experiencing and that feeling of not being good enough by overcompensating in their interactions with others so that people can think of them as good.

If you are a type two personality, then you're more likely to be an emotional sponge always experiencing more than others, which makes you really good at supporting and giving to others. But you might have realized it's somewhat tricky giving to yourself or taking time to tend to your needs. You need to be careful not to absorb emotions on autopilot, as that will destabilize your sense of groundedness. You are a caring, communicative and naturally generous person but you must make sure it's not happening from a place of dependency.

How to self-improve:

Make self-care and self-love a priority in your life. Train yourself to start paying attention to your own needs. I know saying no and setting boundaries is difficult but you need to start recognizing when to set limits for your own mental, emotional, spiritual and physical protection.

Your Wings

The One Wing:

Gifts:
Some of the gifts this wing brings to the helpful giver type include but aren't limited to the following.
- You might feel more influenced to be more generous and giving not just to things you favor but to all things in general.

- You'll firm up your boundaries, get more honest with yourself and instead of exploding, you may find yourself redirecting those emotions to improve things in your surrounding.

Challenges:
Some of the challenges this wing brings to the helpful giver type include but aren't limited to the following.
- The influence of this wing may cause you to overwork yourself in an attempt to help the underdog and bring about more justice.

- You might experience an increase of hurt and a more significant build-up of criticism and resentment.

The Three Wing:

Gifts:
Some of the gifts this wing brings to the helpful giver type include but aren't limited to the following.

- This wing will bring you an increased sense of self-esteem; focus, effectiveness, organization and it will enable you to become a better delegator.

- You will feel confident to hold your own as well as become part of a team. It helps you realize that you don't have to do everything all on your own.

Challenges:
Some of the challenges this wing brings to the helpful giver type include but aren't limited to the following.

- As you become more involved with work and less with your inner self, you might end up neglecting your needs and becoming a workaholic.

- You might also develop the tendency to become acknowledged and be seen as "important" by those you consider influential. Hence the danger of too much pride as the motive for your work.

Type Three: The Achiever also called the Performer

An achiever, also commonly called the performer is the term given to type three personality. While there are some similarities between type one and three, a person in this category is more driven by success and having the best in life. He or she wants to be admired and validated.

Type threes are hard workers, diligent and at times even a little obsessive which is excellent because it keeps them going until they accomplish their goals. Being the best is something this personality type really cares about, and that's why they'll often become the peak performers in their chosen industry. In our modern world, individuals like Muhammad Ali, Will Smith, Tom Cruise, Elon Musk and Oprah Winfrey would undoubtedly be classified as achievers.

The qualities possessed by this person can be outstanding, and it can also be quite harmful if focused on the wrong thing. The desire to be the best at work, look good, demonstrate success and always win can make a type three super competitive, tense and might even lead to him or her to step over others just to get ahead.

Certain qualities are attributed to this type three such as driven, self-confident, image-conscious, adaptable, focused, determined, excellent, energetic and great at leadership and communication.

A type three loves learning, taking on new challenges and winning. This personality type loves to look good and is usually a smart and wonderful person to learn from especially if you want to excel in life too. They have a lot of energy and enthusiasm for life that many find contagious, and this really aids them while rising up the ranks in life or become self-made successes.

They too fall into the Thinking Center which means shame is an underlying emotional theme they continuously have to deal with. Because the three is so focused on image and outward success, he or she usually has a hard time knowing how to handle emotions, especially shame. So denial is often the preferred option for type threes.

Their coping mechanism for shame is striving to become what they believe is the most valuable and successful individual they can possibly be, in the hopes that this will dissolve that underlying restlessness and feelings of shame and inadequacy.

If you are a type three personality then productivity, high performance, and excellence move the needle for you. You love being the best and receiving recognition for it. Forward momentum, being motivated and motivating others around you to succeed comes naturally to you. There's no doubt about it, you think different, dream bigger than most and strive to accomplish more than most people. Your energy is often contagious, and people usually love being around you because you fire them up.

How to self-improve:

Take some time to self-audit regularly and gain clarity on what real success and happiness mean for you. Looking inside might be a little scary, but that's where your real power lies.

It's essential not to confuse material success with fulfillment and self-worth, and you need to draw your power from the real Source of life, not agency power. Your true value cannot come from titles, awards and external validation. And that deep sense of meaning that you long for in your life will not come from accomplishments which is why taking the time to go within and find out who you really are will enable you to emerge better and more prosperous in every conceivable way.

Your Wings

The Two Wing:

Gifts:
Some of the gifts this wing brings to the competitive achiever include but aren't limited to the following.

- This wing actually gives you the gift of finding that balance between being task or goal oriented and caring about the people. It enables you to value people and the contribution they make in your life.

- You also become more aware of your needs and see the value of prioritizing non-work relations.

Challenges:
Some of the challenges this wing brings to the competitive achiever include but aren't limited to the following.

- You may experience a lot more disappointment and self-criticism if your achievements are not appreciated.

- You might also have an increased need for validation and gaining the approval of others especially those that are key stakeholders. Pleasing people might take a toll on your actions.

The Four Wing:

Gifts:
Some of the gifts this wing brings to the competitive achiever include but aren't limited to the following.

- One of the best gifts you will receive from this wing is the realization that self-development and taking time to understand the inner world has tremendous value.

- You will feel an increased need to be authentic, true to yourself and value relationships as a mutual exchange.

Challenges:
Some of the challenges this wing brings to the competitive achiever include but aren't limited to the following.

- You might find yourself being more moody, introverted and overly reflective.

- The amplifying feeling that "something is missing" may cause you to jump from one intense and short-lived relationship to another to help you feel good.

Type Four: The Romantic also called the Individualist

A type four person is mostly referred to as the individualist, but I also like the term romantic.

This person is super creative, sees beauty and magnificence in everything and tends to romanticize things. Think of famous individuals like Oscar Wilde, Michael Jackson, William Shakespeare or the Persian poet Hafiz, and you now have a better idea of people who would fall into this type.

Character qualities associated with this personality type include creativity, authenticity, courage, passion and emotional depth.

However, they are also considered very temperamental, self-absorbed and dramatic, always exaggerating things. There's an underlying sense of melancholy to type fours because they invariably feel like something is missing.

Fours long to be understood and treasured for who they really are but regularly feel misunderstood and unappreciated. Such a person will build an internal mental landscape where it feels more liberating and nourishing as a means of escaping the harsh, cruel world that never "gets them" or their sensitivities.

It has been said that most fours are artistic or very much into art as a means of self-expression, but whether this is the case or not, a type four personality will tend to experience a lot of displeasure and dissatisfaction in the world since they feel different and unique from those who are not like them. And they will seek to find and express wholeness and beauty in some idealistic way.

Being the most emotional of all personality types, they tend to struggle the most with the dominant emotional theme of shame. They are part of the Feeling Center and they unquestionably "feel" deeply, so their discomfort is probably more pronounced and easier to spot. However, they do try to mask this by focusing on how unique and special they are even though it may result in rollercoaster experiences of plunging into a deep depression and other negative emotions to the other extreme of beauty, joy, fantasy and inspired creativity.

If you are a personality type four, then you value individualism and personal self-expression. You love seeing someone authentically sharing their feelings, yet you notice that at times you can be really warm and welcoming while at other times you can become dry and almost cold to people. One day you can be ecstatic and soon after plunge right into depression. Envy and jealousy often creep up on you even though you don't like admitting it even to yourself.

How to self-improve:

That inner critic that's often so loud needs to be tamed and put on mute. Internalizing blame is very unhealthy for you and requires a shift in your perception and how you process negative emotions and situations.

Learn to speak your truth openly without losing control of your emotions. Find a way to balance your emotional rollercoaster so you can stop falling into the pit of despair and depression.

Your Wings

The Two Wing:

Gifts:
Some of the gifts this wing brings to the creative, intense individualist type include but aren't limited to the following.

- The desire to be successful and look good that comes organically from this wing actually helps you to be real and resist being a drama queen or king.

- It also helps you feel more compelled to self-express in a practical way motivating you to be more active, creative and productive work that engages and inspires others. In short, you're more capable of balancing your inner and outer world.

Challenges:
Some of the challenges this wing brings to the creative, intense individualist type include but aren't limited to the following.

- There is a tendency to want to fix others and the external world instead of yourself.

- You are more prone to agitation and depression as the continued pressure to perform and become successful is added to your melancholic personality type.

The Five Wing:

Gifts:
Some of the gifts this wing brings to the creative, intense individualist type include but aren't limited to the following.

- Your highly sensitive, intuitive and emotional personality type gets balanced out with reason, logic and objective observation.
- As thinking is merged with feeling, you will become less impulsive, dramatic and more self-controlled.

Challenges:
Some of the challenges this wing brings to the creative, intense individualist type include but aren't limited to the following.

- When having tough times or feeling depressed, you'll most likely isolate yourself and hide your emotions from others.

- You might also struggle to connect with others and feel marginalized like some kind of alien around others.

Type Five: The Observer also called the Investigator

The Observer personality, also commonly referred to as the investigator is usually brilliant, highly intellectual, keen to continuously learn and feels most comfortable in the realm of thought. This type of person tends to be very independent and enjoys solitude. He or she likes to gather information and observe patterns all around them trying to make sense of their environment and world. Individuals like Albert Einstein, Nikola Tesla, Isaac Newton, and Marie Curie are a few examples of people in this type.

Some of the qualities associated with type fives are innovative, self-reliant, isolated, secretive, curious, perceptive, scholarly, quiet and reserved. They are intense, smart thinkers and take great pleasure tending to the affairs of their mind instead of trying to fit into the world.

As the mental-based types, fives will often detach from relationships, and many consider them emotionally unexpressive. But not all of them. Some fives do care about family and relationships, but even they require a lot of time alone to recreate themselves and pursue their passions. It's not easy figuring out what's going on beneath the surface level of a five and they have an exaggerated need for privacy.

The type five personality falls into the group of the 'Thinking Center' making fear one of the dominant negative themes they have to deal with. Fear of inadequacy is one of the great battles a five must overcome when it comes to dealing with the external world as they feel unable to handle the external world actively.

Perhaps this is why they tend to be detached from others and their own feelings.

Expert says that fives like to withdraw from the world due to their unconscious fear and a belief that by going into their minds and using that to penetrate the nature of our society they can better relate to it. Unfortunately, that usually doesn't work out too well for them and in their fear of being overwhelmed by people or emotions they may come across as arrogant and dismissive.

If you're a type five, then you probably value knowledge and continued education a lot especially in the topics that interest you. Some people think you're overly intellectual and sometimes you can be quite literal, but you don't really care.

Small talk and gossip annoy you to bits, and you prefer solitude. You tend to get stuck in your head, and you prefer hanging out with people who give you enough room to think things over. You like to be thorough in all that you do, and you enjoy very much engaging in deep, meaningful conversations. In fact, when you're passionate about something, you can talk about it in great technical details for a very long time. Reconnecting with the sensations and energy within your body and heart is quite a task even though you know it's good for you and above all else, personal freedom and autonomy bring you great pleasure.

How to self-improve:

Start by increasing the amount of time you spend reconnecting with your body and emotions. Your ability to access your energy and higher spiritual perceptions will only make you stronger.

Create a safe environment for yourself where you can embark on this quest regularly so that you can merge your intellectual strength with your spiritual power.

Put a little more effort on the relationships you care about.

Let your loved ones know that you care about them and be more expressive of your feelings even if it feels a little uncomfortable. Allow yourself to "feel" emotions like joy, being in love, gratitude, affection and so on. This will open up a channel for others to pour in the same into your life and help you deal with the feelings of loneliness and inadequacy that sometimes resurface.

Your Wings

The Two Wing:

Gifts:
Some of the gifts this wing brings to the quiet expert type include but aren't limited to the following.

• For a type five personality, you will have the unusual ability to connect your right and left-brain making you both intuitive and analytical.

• You will also connect more deeply in your intimate relationships.

Challenges:
Some of the challenges this wing brings to the quiet expert type include but aren't limited to the following.

• You might end up withdrawing even further from the material world and get lost in mental fantasies.

• This wing could bring with it an amplified sense of being misunderstood and feeling like no one "gets you." This could lead to mood disorders and even depression.

The Six Wing:

Gifts:
Some of the gifts this wing brings to the quiet expert include but aren't limited to the following.

- You will have the ability to connect more deeply with groups or teams that you trust.

- This wing brings with it the courage and assertiveness of the type six, which can be very useful for you when dealing with everyday living.

Challenges:
Some of the challenges this wing brings to the quiet expert include but aren't limited to the following.

- There is a tendency to be very indecisive and fearful which could make you hesitant about getting involved in new projects or with new people.

- An increase of skepticism coming organically from this wing may have a very negative influence on your core personality causing you to be even more withdrawn and isolated from others.

Type Six: The Doubter also called the Loyal skeptic

A type six personality is always alert and keenly aware of their environment and their responsibilities. Knowing the rules and safeguarding those under their care is super important to sixes. They are very trustworthy and value being there for the people they care about. Unfortunately, they tend to feel conflicted between trusting and distrusting others. They often bounce between skepticism and certainty with a tendency to doubt themselves and question others.

They are very sober-minded people and take problem solving rather seriously to the point where it becomes a burden for them. Worry and anxiety are prevalent emotions for a six. Peace of mind is always lacking in this type, and they usually struggle with a deep sense of insecurity. If you want an idea of celebrities that could be classified as type six individuals, then think of Ellen DeGeneres, Tom Hanks, and Richard Nixon.

Some of the character qualities associated with a type six include trustworthy, responsible, committed, loyal and dependable.

The six also falls into the 'Thinking center' making fear (which often shows up as worry and anxiety) the more dominant emotional theme to watch for.

When a type six personally doesn't put their fear in check, they tend to become really suspicious of everything.

Stress levels are always high for a six and worry seems to be a constant companion as their outlook on life is often quite negative. They will dwell more on the negatives than the positives of any given situation.

If you are a type six, then you tend to pay close attention to people and problems. You're really good at anticipating problems and creating solutions, and you tend not to like ambiguity in others. But you may have realized that you can become very pessimistic, doubtful and even project some of your fears on other people. Sometimes you like to play the devil's advocate. As you grow, it's becoming more important to overcome the mind-body disconnect and even though you're cautious (maybe even phobic), you also demonstrate a lot of courage as you try to move forward even when fear has a hold on you.

How to self-improve:

Find ways to deal with the crippling effects of fear in your life and get better at facing it directly. Ask for some help and support either from an expert or trusted friend.

Learn to take things with a light heart.
Reconnect more with your body and feelings and create a safe space from which to do this so that your mental processes can be relaxed and aid in this new experiment. The more comfortable and safe you feel mentally, the faster and more enjoyable the mind-body connection will become.

Your Wings

The Five Wing:

Gifts:
Some of the gifts this wing brings to the loyal skeptic type include but aren't limited to the following.

- This wing helps you make more reasonable and sound decisions. It also makes you open-minded and capable of taking in multiple perspectives.
- You will also experience a more profound sense of inner trust and confidence in yourself as an observer and authority on your focused interested. This helps eradicate that need to seek validation from others.

Challenges:
Some of the challenges this wing brings to the loyal skeptic type include but aren't limited to the following.

- This wing may amplify your fears and anxiety or any sense of inadequacy you may have.

- You might notice a tendency to be too stuck in your head and not enough alignment with your feelings.

The Seven Wing:

Gifts:
Some of the gifts this wing brings to the loyal skeptic type include but aren't limited to the following.

- The gift of receiving this wing is that you become more optimistic. You start to see more good and become less inclined to imagine the worst of people and the world in general.

- You might notice a shift within, and without in how you approach others, how playful, lighthearted and enthusiastic you feel. It's even possible to become aware of and even laugh at your own fears as you spot them.

Challenges:
Some of the challenges this wing brings to the loyal skeptic type include but aren't limited to the following.

- The common tendency to fear and avoid pain at all cost will be amplified by this wing. This could lead to you seeking all kinds of unhealthy distractions or withdrawing even more from life.

- You might start avoiding confronting issues that require your attention and seek escapism instead.

Type Seven: The Dreamer also called the Enthusiast

The dreamer is spontaneous, a real pleasure seeker and loves to live life to the max.

Having fun is the top priority of this personality type, and they are always looking to catch the next exciting adventure that's just around the corner. Also called enthusiasts or epicures, sevens are mental based types who are forward thinkers and can't stand being limited to doing only one thing. They believe in unlimited possibilities, and it shows their variety of passions and interests. Think of individuals like Steve Jobs, Robert Downey Jr., George Clooney, and Elton John. We believe they would definitely fall into this personality type.

Some of the primary qualities attributed to those in this personality type include enthusiasm, spontaneity, resourceful, adventurous, optimistic fun and exciting.

Some sevens are extroverts though not all and in general are great communicators. Unfortunately being mental based types, they are part of the 'Thinking Center' making the dominant emotional theme of fear their most significant hurdle to overcome. And it shows up for a seven in the form of avoiding pain.

As a pleasure seeker, a seven will do anything to avoid pain and sometimes seeks distractions that turn into overindulgence. But they rationalize and justify this downward tendency just to avoid suffering. Also, since they keep shifting into the next big thing so often, sevens tend to be very scattered making it hard for them to dive deep into any single idea or stay the course in relationships and at work. True devotion is tough for a seven because he or she is such a believer in a futuristic "next big excitement" which makes it tough to narrow down his or her vision and focus wholeheartedly on one thing.

They are usually known as "big talkers" and prone to addiction and overstimulation, which, depending on the body type can be in the form of substance use, gambling, shopping, adventure seeking, or other addictions.

If you're a type seven-person, then you're very resourceful and like to think fast on your feet and switch things up when needed. Multi-tasking is easy for you and you hate the feeling of constriction.

Fun has to be in everything you do because it's who you are. You're definitely a multi-passionate human being so the commonly preached idea of just finding your "one thing" makes no sense to you. You love learning new things and approach life with an optimism that others genuinely admire.

However, you don't really care about "keeping face" or impressing people. You just care about doing your own thing and having an epic time while at it. You can bounce back from negative emotions and situations super fast. Deep down, however, you've come to the realization that you can't stand the experience of pain and it scares you. Negative states of mind, depression, and suffering whether it's your own or others' is unbearable. Introspection isn't something you enjoy, and you do go through cycles of anxiety and despair that drive you to seek out remedies at any cost.

How to self-improve:

Create a safe support structure that can enable you to face your pain, loss, deprivation or any other suffering you've been avoiding. Learn to embrace and reconnect with your inner world.

Be more present in the moment and find your peace of mind and ease without the use of stimulants. I'm not saying it's going to be easy, but you can do it.

With your level of intelligence, resourcefulness, creativity, natural strength and optimism you can be able to gain true freedom and enjoy being the expanding, adventurous human being that you were meant to be while remaining grounded in your true self.

Your Wings

The Six Wing:

Gifts:
Some of the gifts this wing brings to the enthusiast include but aren't limited to the following.

- This wing brings with it the ability for you to be more grounded and present as a seven causing you to work and connect with others in a more mindful and alert way.

- You will also experience a newfound sense of commitment to your chosen course of action, enabling you to explore things with greater depth. It creates a sense of seriousness and grounds your desire for unlimited freedom.

Challenges:
Some of the challenges this wing could bring to the enthusiast include but aren't limited to the following.

- That increased sense of duty could potentially start feeling like a burden.

- Your underlying fears may seem to be amplified, self-doubt could increase, and you might end up feeling guilty when you act irresponsibly or carefree.

The Eight Wing:

Gifts:
Some of the gifts this wing brings to the enthusiast include but aren't limited to the following.

- By leaning more to access the qualities of this wing, you'll become more assertive and step back into your real power in a more grounded way.

- You will develop resilience and in so doing become less afraid of getting hurt.

Challenges:
Some of the challenges this wing brings to the enthusiast include but aren't limited to the following.

- The insatiable urge often carried as a common characteristic of this wing may not work too well for you. If your selfish desires combine with a need for immediate satisfaction, then you could run the risk of going too far in the name of pleasure and gain. Even if it means taking advantage of others to get what you want.

- You might become more self-absorbed and look down on others treating them with a sense of superiority.

Type Eight: The Challenger also called the Leader

The best statement to sum up this personality type is "I am a master of my fate. I am the captain of my soul." Indeed this personality type believes in taking full control and ownership of their lives and being perceived as the powerful, active leader and protector. Justice, fairness, and independence are of great value to a type eight. If wronged, they will fight back with a vengeance.

Eights are body-based types giving them strong physical appetites and powerful instincts. They are bold, active in decision-making, love to be independent and are very intense people. A person typed as an eight will generally desire a grand life, and he or she will be ready and willing to go out and fight for that desire. In our modern world, individuals like Donald Trump; Denzel Washington would probably fall into this personality type. It's probable that Napoleon Bonaparte, Julia Caesar, and Winston Churchill would also be typed as eights.

Some of the qualities attributed to a type eight include, self-confidence, courage, willfulness, decisiveness, power, boldness, generosity and domination.

Eights can be difficult to handle at times especially if their personalities are developed in unhealthy ways. They are grouped in the 'Instinctive Center' making their emotional theme anger. Eights really know how to get angry. They are very quick to anger whenever they don't get their way, or things go wrong. And in the case of unchecked anger or unhealthy personality traits, that anger can quickly turn to rage and physical violence.

They produce a lot of energy, which enables them to approach challenges with the right mental and physical attitude. The one thing an eight cannot stand is a feeling of weakness. Vulnerability (based on how society defines it) is also something a type eight would steer clear of and that makes having a deep and intimate relationship with the type eight kind of hard.

Even in their intimate relationships they still need to feel in control and powerful. When it comes to protecting their family, friends and those under their care, eights are fierce. They will go to the ends of the earth and do whatever it takes to accomplish the mission.

If you are a type eight personality, then you've noticed a tendency within you to be excessive. Some call you bossy though you don't get why. You see it as just being firm, focused, clear, assertive and leading others to victory.

Idleness, weakness, shyness are all things you can't stand in yourself and others, and you prefer when people are direct and confident as they address you. When provoked you can get outraged, and you tend to have a vengeful attitude toward people. But you always maintain an open mind; a positive mindset and you've got an abundance of energy to share with the world. Being controlled by any organization, person or system is simply unacceptable to you, and you prefer to determine your own high standards and execute on reaching them.

How to self-improve:

You have a lot of energy. Probably the most energetic of all the nine types, which means you, need to direct that energy constructively. Incorporate some self-control into your life and don't let anger and aggression remain your automatic reaction just because it's a comfortable habit.

Redefine what vulnerability means to you and learn to receive love and affection. If you need some personal assistance and support, ask for help from someone you trust or hire an expert. This is not a form of weakness. Don't get trapped in that false belief. Improving yourself is a form of strength, and it empowers you to become a better leader and protector.

Your Wings

The Seven Wing:

Gifts:
Some of the gifts this wing brings to the active controller include but aren't limited to the following.

• Tapping into the gifts of this wing will calm you down, increase your happiness and help you move through life more enthusiastically. It gives you a light heart and dissolves some of that ruthlessness often ruling your life.

• Instead of being a lone wolf trying to make it all on your own, you will start to value connecting with other people, exchanging ideas, expressing your thoughts as well as acting out your fantasies in a more harmonious way.

Challenges:
Some of the challenges this wing could bring to the active controller type include but aren't limited to the following:

• The influence this wing may have on you could make you prone to addictions and overindulgence.

• You might also become too self-absorbed, reckless and less reflective on the consequences of your actions.

The Nine Wing:

Gifts:
Some of the gifts this wing brings to the active controller type include but aren't limited to the following.

- One of the principal gifts this wing could bring into your core personality tendency of being impulsive and autonomous is a renewed sense of unity, balance and being a bit more laid back about things.

- You will become calmer, receptive to others and instead of forcing things to happen, you'll be more at ease with just letting things unfold naturally.

Challenges:
Some of the challenges this wing brings to the active controller type include but aren't limited to the following:

- The influence of the nine wing could lead to a build-up of tension between an increased need to withdraw from people and tasks, but then feeling guilty about it and judging yourself for doing so.

- You might fall into the trap of working too much to the point of unhealthy self-sacrifice and self-neglect.

Type Nine: The Peacemaker also called the Diplomat

The type nine personality is generally known to "go with the flow" in life. They value harmony, peace, and balance above all else and do anything possible to avoid conflict and rivalry. Individuals such as the Dalai Lama, Queen Elizabeth II, Abraham Lincoln, and Grace Kelly are all great examples of people in this personality type.

Some of the essential qualities associated with this personality type include tolerance, sturdiness, reliability, groundedness, calmness, and goodwill.

Nines are body-based types that love to get along with everyone and are pretty awesome to be around because of their friendly, warm nature. Nines can tolerate a lot and usually take an optimistic approach to every situation. They like to see the best in others and have strong faith that things will always work out for the best. They believe in a friendly universe and want to keep an open mind and heart as much as possible.

They are grouped in the 'Instinctive Center' making anger their dominant emotional theme to watch out for. All that calmness can turn into something dark and unhealthy if left unchecked. And it mostly happens in the form of suppressed and denied emotions.

Due to the inherent desire to be a peacemaker in the world, a nine usually denies the threating emotions of anger that surge up every so often. They are the most out of touch with their instinctual drives and dominant emotions within this cluster. The need to avoid conflict at all cost (including internal conflict) causes them to gloss over their unpleasant hidden feelings. A nine is also prone to inaction and procrastination especially when he or she senses unpleasant emotions.

If you're a type nine personality, then you value connecting deeply with the world and those you care about. You tend to take a conservative approach to change and sometimes struggle with a lack of motivation. Being out in nature gives you the most satisfying sensation; it's where you feel most at home.

People consider you warm, nurturing, dependable and attentive. However, this tendency to self-sacrifice carries some significant disadvantages that you don't like facing up to as it brings about discomfort. You may notice that people start taking you for granted or undervalue all that you do for them and it can be very disheartening. You have a tendency to "forget yourself" since you easily merge with others making personal boundaries really hard for you to create.

How to self-improve:

Challenge yourself to take more risks in life. Create a safe space in your life where you can train yourself to integrate harmony and conflict so that you can stop avoiding them all the time.

Pay more attention to your own needs and learn to set clear boundaries. Reconnect with your emotions and embrace the discomfort of conflict or anger as it shows up within you so you can boldly deal with it. Seek to release rather than suppress the negative emotions that do show up. Give yourself time and space to process all your feelings.

Be more structured and strategic with your top priorities. If getting more organized is an issue then ask for help or acquire one of the many modern tools to help you better prioritize activities on a day-to-day basis.

Your Wings

The Eight Wing:

Gifts:
Some of the gifts this wing brings to the adaptive peacemaker include but aren't limited to the following.

- The positive influence this wing brings to your core personality, as a peacemaker is that you'll be more in touch with your power, independence, and authority.

- You'll become more bold, confident, influential and capable of speaking up and expressing your truth.

Challenges:
Some of the challenges this wing brings to the adaptive peacemaker include but are not limited to the following:

- There is a tendency to drift off your right path when under the influence of this wing and you might find yourself pursuing pleasure rather than genuine desires and the needs of your real self.

- You might also experience a lot of explosive aggression, rebelliousness, and anger especially if there have been unresolved issues with authority in the past.

The One Wing:

Gifts:

Some of the gifts this wing brings to the adaptive peacemaker include but aren't limited to the following.

- Your laid back, easy going approach will get an upgrade once you access this wing. It will help you create some structure around your life and activities. You'll develop a more focused perspective and lead a principle-based life.

- You will feel empowered enough to be more actively engaged in changing the things that are going wrong instead of accepting dysfunction as the standard way of life. You'll be more action oriented, but it will come from a place of purpose and certainty.

Challenges:
Some of the challenges this wing brings to the adaptive peacemaker include but aren't limited to the following:

- The increased need to do what's right and make the world perfect may lead to even more procrastination and distraction. The fear of not getting it right might actually become a huge obstacle.

- You might get caught up in the trap of doing what you "should do" or what is expected of you rather than what you really want to do.

Section III: Instincts, Subtypes and variants within the Enneagram of Personality Tool

Chapter 07: Diving Deeper into who you really are

Just like animals, we as human beings have natural instincts hard-wired biologically that help us navigate life. Our evolution has necessitated we develop strategies that will enable us to survive and extend the reign of our species. What the Enneagram of personality does is facilitate a better understanding of the instinctual strategies we've developed as human beings, and it shows us the various ways it's impacting out behavior. This is more than just getting to know your personality type; it's about pulling back the curtain of the influences that drive you to behave as you do.

The Enneagram teachers there are three basic human instincts, and out of these three, we see a detailed dissection of how these instincts interact and combine with the nine personality types to form what is generally referred to by some teachers as the 27 subtypes. These are:

- Self-preservation Instinct.
- Social Instinct.
- Sexual Instinct.

All three instincts are within us and are behind our life strategies often ruling unconsciously. While these three are always present, one tends to be more dominant, and we tend to priorities and develop that particular drive while the others tend to be less dominant. And because we don't make it a priority to improve the least dominant one, it tends to become our blind spot.

Think of these three instincts as you would a layered cake. At the top we have our most controlling one, in the middle, we have the second that supports the predominant one, and at the bottom, we have the least developed instinct.

Again, we find some conflict even here with some schools stating they should not be referred to as subtypes while others teach they are indeed subtypes of the nine-point system. Either way, the label doesn't matter to us. We only concern ourselves with how this can help us better understand who we are and why we behave as we do. The primary instinct that we identify with combined with our Enneagram personality type help shape our path in life and the choices we make.

Since that is our core focus, we'll dive into each of the twenty-seven combinations after a brief understanding of what each instinct entails.

Self-preservation Instinct:

The need to preserve our body and its life force. Keeping away from threats. This includes our basic human needs of food, shelter, clothing, warmth and family relations.

This instinct is very focused on physical well-being, safety, material security, and daily comfort. Whenever our basic needs feel threatened by the environment, we may resort to hoarding of resources and energy to conserve what we have as a result of the external threat. We may consider this the basic primal instincts that all creatures possess as well. The drive to survive and sustain ourselves.

Social Instinct:

This Social instinct is also called "the adaptive" instinct.
It is the need to get along with others and form secure social bonds. It's about creating a sense of belonging around you.

We are seeing this a lot on social media today with memberships and communities popping up where like-minded people (who feel the need to belong) gather together. It's about focusing energy on working towards shared purposes or the greater good.

This instinct is very much about being part of something that resonates with you where you feel secure, heard and valued within that group and community.

Sexual Instinct:

The Sexual instinct is also called "the attraction" instinct.
It is the universal need to procreate and pass on our genes to continue the human race generation after generation. It governs our sexuality, intimacy and the close friendships that we treasure.

This instinct is also about directing the vitality of the life force within our bodies. It focuses on the intensity and passion contained in experiences and one on one relationships which causes us to seek opportunities that promise strong alliances, synergy, and deep connections.

This instinct is often constricted to just sexual intimacy, but it's meant to be so much more than that. It's definitely about projecting yourself into the environment and experiencing intimate relationships that are pleasurable and extend your DNA, but it can also be about passing on ideas that help you create a legacy that continues far beyond your physical reach.

When we overlay these three instincts of human behavior with all that we've discussed so far, the end result is a combination of twenty-seven subtypes further helping you relate to your personality. The set of combination that falls into our most dominant personality type helps us connect to the intricacies of our everyday behavior and preferences.

"These instincts relate to fundamental instinctual intelligence that develops within each of us to ensure our survival as individuals and as a human species.

Recent advances in neuroscience research have confirmed the strong and often invisible way these instincts show up in modern society, for example, how a perceived threat to social status can trigger a primal fight or flight reaction."

(27 Subtypes Integrative 9 Enneagram Solutions - https://www.integrative9.com/enneagram/27-subtypes/)

Self Preservation Instinct	Social Instinct	Sexual Instinct
The need to preserve our body and its life force. Keeping away from threats. This includes our basic human needs of food, shelter, clothing, warmth and family relations.	The need to get along with others and form secure social bonds. It's about creating a sense of belonging around you.	The universal need to procreate and continue the human race generation after generation. It governs our sexuality, intimacy and the close friendships that we treasure as well as our legacy.
Type 1: The Perfectionist /Reformer • Anxiety	**Type 1: The Perfectionist /Reformer** • Non-adaptability	**Type 1: The Perfectionist /Reformer** • Zealousness or Jealousy
Type 2: The Giver/Helper • Privilege	**Type 2: The Giver/Helper** • Ambition	**Type 2: The Giver/Helper** • Seduction or Aggression
Type 3: The Achiever/Performer • Security	**Type 3: The Achiever/Performer** • Prestige	**Type 3: The Achiever/Performer** • Charisma
Type 4: The Romantic/Individualist • Fearlessness	**Type 4: The Romantic/Individualist** • Shame	**Type 4: The Romantic/Individualist** • Competition
Type 5: The Observer/Investigator • Castle	**Type 5: The Observer/Investigator** • Symbols	**Type 5: The Observer/Investigator** • Confidant
Type 6: The Loyalist/Doubter • Warmth	**Type 6: The Loyalist/Doubter** • Duty	**Type 6: The Loyalist/Doubter** • Warrior
Type 7: The Enthusiast/Dreamer • Networking	**Type 7: The Enthusiast/Dreamer** • Sacrifice	**Type 7: The Enthusiast/Dreamer** • Fascination

1. Personality Type One: The Perfectionist also called the Reformer

- **Self-preservation Instinct:**

The fundamental character drive here will be projected as Anxiety.

This is the perfectionist who constantly worries and seeks to control everything. Their anxiety causes them to try to anticipate risks constantly, and they like to be very prepared for everything. Attention to detail is probably an understatement for them. They are usually very hard on themselves and take things rather seriously.

This subtype prefers to avoid expressing anger even if they feel it and they will often experience and demonstrate great frustration when interrupted. The type one subtype has a very loud inner critic and tends to amplify their worry and anxiety.

- **Social Instinct:**

The fundamental character drive here will be projected as Non-adaptability.

Fairness and making things right motivate this subtype. They are systematic thinkers, set high standards for themselves and others and like to be an example of integrity and principled conduct.

They practice a lot of self-control and can be quite friendly while in their own comfort zone. Because they are so linear and see everything in black and white; right or wrong, it can be tough adapting to a new environment or situation. They can also become very resentful and critical with those who don't fit their idea of right.

- **Sexual Instinct:**

The fundamental character drive here will be projected as Zealousness and/or Jealousy.

This subtype will be highly charged, passionate and maintain high standards of self-control. They have an idealistic view of how things should be and have a tendency of wanting to reform others and make them fit into "what's right."

Rage and anger will directly be expressed by those who fall into this subtype, mainly if their efforts to improve others are restricted. They also prioritize holding the attention of their partner and usually become very jealous toward their partner or when dealing with others who seem to be doing better.

2. Personality Type Two: The Giver also called the Helper

- Self-preservation Instinct:

The fundamental character drive here will be projected as Privilege.

This type two feels privileged and unique in some way because he or she invests a lot in the creation of warm nurturing relationships. They spend a lot of time caring for and supporting others. As such there's a tendency to become self-entitled and even develop a prideful attitude demanding special privileges and approval as a result of the caretaking.

They are "cute" with a highly activated child-like spirit. This type two likes being taken care of but isn't too keen on long-term commitments. Fear of rejection is a big deal for this subtype, and they can experience a lot of hurt and abandonment when their needs are not met.

- Social Instinct:

The fundamental character drive here will be projected as Ambition.

Forming the right alliances and having great allies is essential for this subtype because they like to build their self-esteem through visible accomplishments and social approval.

This type two will use his or her seductive powers more intellectually to attune to others' needs and create a role that is central and almost indispensable within the organization, community or broader system. They like to stand out from the crowd and enjoy taking on leadership roles. They relish "being switched on" and build their influence based on the connections they form as well as their competencies.

Those in this subtype do not actively demonstrate a child-like spirit (at least not as much as the other type twos) and tend to have a strategy of giving more than they get. Seeking recognition through ambition is more pronounced in this type two personality.

- **Sexual Instinct:**

The fundamental character drive here will be projected as Seduction and/ or aggression.

This type two will focus all their energies, skills and seductive abilities to form and nurture powerful and intimate relationships.
This type of person is passionate, resilient, strong-willed and at times may be considered wild at heart. They are very devoted in their personal relationships, and they don't like taking no for an answer.

This type two uses seduction, which can go as far as turning into aggression if pushed into it, to gain the desired attention and recognition.
Although they like to use body language and feeling tones that may come across as seductive, it doesn't necessarily imply sexual desire.

3. The Achiever also called the Performer

- **Self-preservation Instinct:**

The fundamental character drive here will be projected as Security.

This type three variation is very focused on achievement and creating material success for himself or herself. This type of person avoids being seen as image-oriented and does not like advertising his or her strengths overtly. But being successful and getting recognition for their hard work is still super important to them. Financial success and creating a sense of security around them is a huge priority for this subtype.

They work very hard and like to maintain high standards and the right image of success. This subtype three has an abundance of energy and tends to accomplish a lot.

The real danger for them is the fact that in chasing after all that success, they often lose contact with their authentic self and are prone to creating false identities and valuing themselves based on their job role or social status.

- **Social Instinct:**

The fundamental character drive here will be projected as Prestige.

This type three variation is more interested in being validated and receiving lots of social approval. They crave power, work hard to "know the right people" and focus a lot in gaining powerful leadership positions in the government or in business.

Prestige, praise, and influence are what this subtype will be after the most, and he or she will generally train themselves to adjust to the social norms and requirements of teams or organizations if it helps them gain influence and power. They are highly competitive and love being in the spotlight.

This particular subtype will have no issues confidently promoting their ideas and accomplishments. Unlike the first type three who would rather not advertise their achievements and success, this subtype would actually go to the extreme to make theirs known. And to cover up anything that doesn't align with that "perfect success image."

- **Sexual Instinct:**

The fundamental character drive here will be projected as Charisma.

Personal power and gender identification as well as all the issues that arise from that mostly drive this type three variation. Masculinity and femininity matter a lot to them. Having the life of a "movie star" which means having that perfect outer image is what rocks their world. They are also very enthusiastic and charismatic which makes them very likable.

Being attractive to others as a man or woman is super important. But they do enjoy supporting others in their success as well and often posses that enthusiastic attitude "if you succeed, then I succeed."

The biggest challenge for this subtype despite remaining very competitive, charismatic and powerful on the outside is that those who fall into the unhealthy path of their subtype will often struggle silently with feelings of confusion concerning their sexuality. It can be tough to deal with such conflicts since so much effort is placed on appearing like a powerful performer.

4. The Romantic also called the Individualist.

- Self-preservation Instinct:

The fundamental character drive here will be projected as Fearlessness.

This type four variation while still very sensitive and idealistic will express their emotions less. In a sense, we could say they are the least dramatic of the three subtypes. But that doesn't mean they do not experience those tumultuous emotions, they just want to be viewed as someone who doesn't complain.

The truth is this type of person has simply trained himself or herself to live with suffering and pain. They know how to internalize negative emotions and prefer to be tough enough to deal with whatever comes. It makes them least likely to open up and share their feelings with others in comparison to the other subtypes, but that doesn't mean they lack in empathy. In fact, they try very hard to reach out to and support those who are suffering around them.

This subtype is very creative and deeply craves to experience an authentic life even if that means being a bit reckless at times. They will have no trouble packing up and moving to an entirely new environment if their self-preservation trigger makes them feel like an authentic experience is elsewhere.

The biggest challenge for this personality type variation is the tension often created between the desire to build material security in their lives while still remaining fully detached from it all.

- **Social Instinct:**

The fundamental character drive here will be projected as Shame.

This subtype is profoundly emotional and highly tuned into their own sense of suffering. A person in this subtype will actually find comfort in suffering and expressing it to others. This tends to generate attention, support and at times admiration from others.

They often feel inadequate around social situations and easily get envious of other people's social status or when they encounter those who seem like they've already found a place where they "belong." A sense of belonging really drives them, and they strive to establish an acceptable social role where they can be heard as they share their truth.

This subtype is not competitive at all, but they do have a great desire to be understood and seen for who they really are. Their biggest issue is being able to overcome the social shame they often experience, and because they constantly doubt themselves and struggle with feelings of inferiority, there's always a hidden inner conflict going on. A person in this subtype will notice he or she has a tendency to blame others, compare themselves to others and constantly struggle with deep shame and envy.

- **Sexual Instinct:**

The fundamental character drive will be competition.
If the previous subtype can be termed shameful, then this variation of the personality may be called 'shameless.'

This subtype is very loud and vocal about having their needs met. They express their emotions and desires with lots of vigor. It's what I call the classic drama queen or king. They are super demanding and highly competitive. Because they believe in evaluating themselves based on how they match up to other people, competition is a big motivation for this subtype, and they will do anything to beat the competition.

Unfortunately, this competitiveness comes from a place of deep-seated insecurity and feelings of inadequacy. Personal blocks and issues are always resurfacing for this subtype because their sense of worth and value is directly tied to being able to beat those they consider strong and powerful.

5. The Observer also called the Investigator.

- **Self-preservation Instinct:**

The fundamental character drive here will be projected in the form of The Castle.

This personality variation is driven by the need to be very protective of the place they call home. Their personal space and privacy are very much off limits, and they have no trouble setting clear boundaries for everyone. They enjoy living a comfortable and relatively solitary life with just a few close friends.

A person in this subtype would rather sit back and observe social life than actively participate in it. They are very guarded and independent opting to cut off intimacy so as not to lower their guard and lose that sense of privacy and safety.

It's essential for this subtype to have a safe haven where they can retreat and take refuge from the world. And because they also like seclusion, having enough supplies is always a concern for them, which often leads to hoarding and living a minimalist lifestyle.

Some subtypes, however, go to the other extreme and chose to make their 'castle' wherever they are and end up traveling forever or moving from place to place. They tend to be introverts, though not all and prefer not to reveal much of their inner world.

- Social Instinct:

The fundamental character drive here will be projected in the form of Symbols.

This personality type variation is brilliant and hungry for more knowledge. Their main focus is seeking meaning and answers to the more significant questions of life. They take little to no pleasure dealing with daily trivia. Their hunger for mastery and understanding sacred symbols and language leads them down paths ordinary human beings rarely traverse.

This subtype loves to connect with and engage other brilliant minds and experts who share their ideas and hunger for higher knowledge and wisdom. Unfortunately, they often get too stuck in too much critical thinking, analysis and interpretation causing a snag in their ability to participate with others actively.

A person in this subtype will tend to be very private, reclusive and quiet, unwilling to share their personal space or inner resources but at the same time when triggered to speak on a topic they are passionate about, the same person can become very animated, speak lengthily and with great enthusiasm. It's almost as though they can go from being entirely introverted to energetically extroverted at the push of a button.

- Sexual Instinct:

The fundamental character drive here will be projected in the form of The Confidant.

This type five variation is the one related to person and connectedness the most. They too love keeping things confidential but with this slight alteration. A subtype five confidant will open up and share intimate information about their inner world and frame of mind in a private one-on-one relationship. But only to a chosen few who first undergo a series of loyalty tests.

This subtype possesses the more cool and analytical character traits and although still super secretive and reserved, once they do find that "shared chemistry" with another they will open up and enjoy the trust and connection such a relationship permits.

The primary challenge this subtype struggles with is the tension created between profoundly connecting with another person and the need to preserve autonomy.

6. The Doubter also called the Loyalist.

- Self-preservation Instinct:

The fundamental character drive here will be projected as Warmth.

This type six variation is very affectionate and warm-hearted. But fear, anxiety, and insecurity are very pronounced in them. They attempt to overcome it by forming strong relationships and bonds that help them feel secure.

Often you'll find an earlier childhood event may have created a lot of suppressed hurt causing them to be very fearful of risk-taking or making mistakes. As a result, this subtype will prefer to repress their negative emotions especially anger because they view that as a better and more cautious way of dealing with such feelings especially if they believe it might jeopardize the warmth in a relationship they genuinely need.

A person in this subtype doesn't like feeling "left out" and struggles with openly sharing their opinions. He or she prefers to stay within well-established boundaries, and risk-taking doesn't come easy.

- Social Instinct:

The fundamental character drive here will be projected as A Sense of Duty.

This type six personality variation is very focused on and concerned about living up to one's own duty. Integrity, fairness, and responsibility matter a lot to those who belong to this subtype. They believe in standing up for "the little guy" and defending the weak.

This subtype is highly rational and devoted to their work, choosing to follow the rules and procedures set in their environment. They tend to be more black and white, connect to social ideals and enjoy working toward a greater cause.

A person in this subtype is very concerned about knowing the rules and making sure that everyone understands their role too often creating clear agreements with colleagues and friends to avoid confusion or unnecessary squabble. The great challenge is the fear of rejection often brewing underneath and the deep sense of responsibility carried by their own duty which can either become a calling or a burden to them depending on how they develop their personality.

- **Sexual Instinct:**

The fundamental character drive here will be projected as The Warrior.

This particular personality type variation has two styles. The first style is based on overcoming the undercurrent of fear through willpower and feats of physical strength and bravery. It could also be seen in gaining intellectual power.

The second style is seen by creating beauty in their environment. Channeling their idealism and keen perceptiveness into the creation of beauty in the hopes that it will help them feel more in control and stable.

Both styles within this subtype indicate a bold assertiveness, which often passes for intimidation. A person in this subtype will unquestionably experience a lot of self-doubt, fear, and instability and will often attempt to avoid or overcome it by running straight toward it either through a focus on strength or beauty. This need for safety and power often clouds their ability to connect to their own emotions and causes them to struggle a lot with vulnerability.

7. The Dreamer also called the Enthusiast.

- Self-preservation Instinct:

The fundamental character drive here will be projected in the form of Networking.

This personality type variation loves to have good things in life and surround themselves with rich relationships, beauty, fun conversations, and entertainment.

They love planning fun projects or events, preparing elaborate meals, dining out, and sharing good ideas and even networking. Although they are more interested in family and friends, their energetic and enthusiastic approach to life and people makes them great at nurturing a "family" relation that extends far beyond blood relatives. What motivates them is making sure everyone is doing well and having the best experience with them.

A person in this subtype is generally very good at getting what they want and justifying or defending what they want to do. The biggest challenge is the tendency to overdo things, become too self-interested or overindulge in some way either with food, talking, shopping or stimulants.

- Social Instinct:

The fundamental character drive here will be projected as Sacrifice.

This subtype tends to act against the common trait of insatiability exhibited by the other sevens. They are generous and have a strong desire to create meaning and make a difference in the world. They are happy to sacrifice their own needs to serve the needs of the group, family, organization or person that they support. They have a utopian outlook on life, which usually serves them really well.

However, there is an underlying current of dependency being experienced with this subtype because they need friends and other people or group based projects to self-express and feel like they are doing something meaningful. In all their self-sacrificing nature they secretly hope to be acknowledged and appreciated for the sacrifices they make.

A person in this subtype is very generous, visionary in their thinking, focuses more on others and is drawn to anything that aims to fulfill a greater cause. Their primary challenge is the tendency to be very judgmental of others and themselves whenever they perceive a sense of selfishness showing up.

- Sexual Instinct:

The fundamental character drive here will be projected as Fascination.

Here we find the classical dreamer and idealist. This personality type variant sees the world through rose-colored filters. He or she is attracted instantly to new ideas, new people and possible adventure falling immediately into a state of fascination. But this suggestibility works both ways.

This subtype not only gets fascinated easily but as well as fascinate others. Their charm can be very persuasive and irresistible making such people great at sales and customer service.

A person in this subtype sees the good in everything and is always enthusiastic and optimistic. He or she is ever connected to the stream of infinite possibilities.

The primary challenge is having to deal with things that he or she considers dull, dreary, boring and predictable. Conditions, people and even a world that's dull are totally unacceptable and become a source of frustration.

8. The Challenger also called the Leader.

- Self-preservation Instinct:

The fundamental character drive here will be projected as Survival.

This personality variation will be more driven and focused on survival and protecting those under their care. More interested in securing physical and material success and security. These subtype eights are aggressive and excessive in their tendencies.

A typical attitude of mind is "win or die fighting." This subtype is usually seen as a very powerful, productive and direct personality never backing out of situations just because things get tough. They are also very fiercely protective of their family and friends and are often perceived as the strong pillar holding things together.

A person in this subtype is confident, secure, powerful, direct and will usually take the role of guardian, father or mother figure. He or she is very concerned with protecting themselves, the space around them and those under their care. Survival is a major concern at all times.

- Social Instinct:

The fundamental character drive here will be projected as camaraderie.

This personality variation of an eight still possesses the same aggression and excessiveness of type eight, but they channel it differently. A sense of injustice and powerlessness is active within the individuals that fall into this subtype, which they attempt to resolve by forming groups or alliances, which they become very devoted to.

They focus more on social causes and prefer to be the leader of the group or alliance, serving the people for a higher mission. Unfairness, injustice or abuse of power really triggers their sensitivities, and they feel the need to protect those under their influence against such things. They prefer to support others rather than assert their own personal needs.

A person in this subtype will usually choose to mediate his or her anger by harnessing that energy to serve the needs of the community members they serve. He or she will also want to be the "shield" loyally protecting his or her tribe from unjust authority or any other type of danger.

- Sexual Instinct:

The fundamental character drive here will be projected as Possessiveness.

This type eight variation demands control over others and loves to possess whatever they desire. They like to be rebellious and aren't afraid to break the rules. Impulsiveness rules for this subtype, and they are usually very intense people always ready to disrupt things and bring about change. They will never shy away from challenging the status quo and have a need to drive change, gain power and influence over others.

When it comes to intimacy, the eights aggression and possessiveness is still very pronounced often wanting to dominate the partner entirely.

A person in this subtype will have the same aggressive and excessive qualities that all type eights have, but with one distinct difference. They will tend to take it a bit too far.

There's a hunger for possession, which can at times be good if it's directed toward serving a worthy cause. But it can also be dangerous if directed toward something detrimental for them and others. Sometimes this personality subtype may be willing to let go and surrender if he or she feels a strong enough yearning from a partner capable of fully meeting their needs.

9. The Peacemaker also called the Diplomat.

- Self-preservation Instinct:

The fundamental character drive here will be projected as a Strong Appetite.

This personality variation is somewhat similar to an eight subtype in that they are very self-focused and concerned about meeting physical needs.
Material security and providing daily comfort for themselves is super important. Those who fall in this subtype have a big appetite for food and possessing things.

A person in this subtype is often a collector. Very focused on fulfilling their personal needs and providing material comfort. He or she loves to have time alone and can become very irritable when someone threatens their sense of balance or disrupts the daily rhythms that support their instinctual life. Material abundance is often more important than personal or spiritual growth.

- Social Instinct:

The fundamental drive will be projected as a Powerful Need for Participation.

This personality variation of the nine is the more friendly, selfless and warm type. Those who are in this subtype are usually strong, reliable, always in harmony with others and do a great job blending in with the agenda of their friends or the different social groups they become part of.

Often showing excellent leadership skills and selfless contribution, this subtype will position themselves as the mediator or facilitator, which comes naturally to them. Being part of a broader group or the community benefactor is their instinctual motive. They don't like burdening others with their personal struggles so they'll usually maintain a happy attitude and focus on the needs of others and their roles.

A person in this subtype is more interested in just feeling like they are participating in something meaningful. He or she works hard to make those they love happy and are very willing to make whatever sacrifices necessary to meet the needs of those under their care.

They are affectionate and amicable doing everything possible to be a reliable, concrete pillar for those in their care even if it means neglecting their own pain and struggles.

- **Sexual Instinct:**

The fundamental character drive here will be projected as Fusion or The Need To Merge.

This personality variation can be best termed as the seeker. Union with others is their instinctual motive, and that can be sexual or spiritual either with another person, nature or life itself.

This deep longing can be chaotic at times, or it can be the doorway to a transcendental experience. They tend to feel more comfortable and secure when partnered with others and usually can't stand being on their own. As a result, there can be a tendency to go along with what others demand and exclude their personal preferences.

A person in this subtype is usually very warm and affectionate possessing a deep urge to merge. Their most significant challenge is making this practical in daily living and keeping personal boundaries as well as the right focus on oneself.

How to know your subtype:

Before moving on to the next section, here are a few tips on how to recognize your subtype. For some people, this might come easy. In a matter of minutes, you could take the Enneagram test and figure out your center as well as your subtypes. If that's you, I'm glad. You're good to go. Just apply everything you've learned as you move forward in life.

If however, you're not that fortunate and still feel lost, confused or even unable to figure out your subtype instantly, I got you covered. You're not alone. This is something that happens to a lot of people. It requires more study and exploration over time, so allow the process to evolve naturally.

To some extent, I think we all identify with all three instinctual drives. So if you find that happening just know there's nothing wrong with you. After all, they all exist in each of us. But which is most vital for you overall? That's the clarity you need.

The enneagram subtypes aren't meant to be an exact science. Instead, they are intended to evoke a specific theme and make you aware of the different seasons in your life and the various motives influencing your choices. The Enneagram personality tool is a dynamic growth-oriented system and is meant to be a personal inventory that aims to pinpoint your basic fears motivations and strengths so you can facilitate your personal growth through a specific trajectory.

If you can start by confidently identifying your primary type and the main center of intelligence (one of the triads), then you'll be able to discover which of the underlying fears guide the majority of your behavior as well as your most dominant instinct.

You might even notice that the theme keeps changing as your living conditions and circumstances change, and that's okay too. Avoid becoming too rigid about this as you determine what to identify with.

Take a look at the diagram I share below. That should give you a visual representation of your subtypes. You may choose to first start by identifying yourself with the instinctual center that draws you in the most. For example: If you genuinely feel you're driven by social instinct and the need for belonging or fighting for a higher cause within a group, then you can focus on the - social instinct- and match your enneagram type with the corresponding subtype.

Self Preservation Instinct	Social Instinct	Sexual Instinct
The need to preserve our body and its life force. Keeping away from threats. This includes our basic human needs of food, shelter, clothing, warmth and family relations.	The need to get along with others and form secure social bonds. It's about creating a sense of belonging around you.	The universal need to procreate and continue the human race generation after generation. It governs our sexuality, intimacy and the close friendships that we treasure as well as our legacy.
Type 1: The Perfectionist /Reformer	**Type 1: The Perfectionist /Reformer**	**Type 1: The Perfectionist /Reformer**
• Anxiety	• Non-adaptability	• Zealousness or Jealousy
Type 2: The Giver/Helper	**Type 2: The Giver/Helper**	**Type 2: The Giver/Helper**
• Privilege	• Ambition	• Seduction or Aggression
Type 3: The Achiever/Performer	**Type 3: The Achiever/Performer**	**Type 3: The Achiever/Performer**
• Security	• Prestige	• Charisma
Type 4: The Romantic/Individualist	**Type 4: The Romantic/Individualist**	**Type 4: The Romantic/Individualist**
• Fearlessness	• Shame	• Competition
Type 5: The Observer/Investigator	**Type 5: The Observer/Investigator**	**Type 5: The Observer/Investigator**
• Castle	• Symbols	• Confidant
Type 6: The Loyalist/Doubter	**Type 6: The Loyalist/Doubter**	**Type 6: The Loyalist/Doubter**
• Warmth	• Duty	• Warrior
Type 7: The Enthusiast/Dreamer	**Type 7: The Enthusiast/Dreamer**	**Type 7: The Enthusiast/Dreamer**
• Networking	• Sacrifice	• Fascination
Type 8: The Challenger/Leader	**Type 8: The Challenger/Leader**	**Type 8: The Challenger/Leader**
• Survival	• Camaraderie	• Possessiveness
Type 9: The Peacemaker/Diplomat	**Type 9: The Peacemaker/Diplomat**	**Type 9: The Peacemaker/Diplomat**
• Strong Appetite	• Participation	• Fusion

If that doesn't seem to be yielding clear results, try another approach. You may choose to write down all the sets of nines within the subtypes that most resonate with you. Out of the sets of nine terms, you'll probably feel more drawn to one than the other two. The one that most draws you in should be the instinctual title that best describes your habits, preoccupations, and anxieties over the long-run.

My friend Joanna struggled at first with identifying her subtype. She thought she was an Enneagram personality type four with the self-preservation instinct as her dominant subtype. Her husband didn't agree. This created some doubt in her, and it took a lot of studies and deep reflection before she finally felt comfortable with her chosen Enneagram type and subtype. Perhaps you will need to do the same at first. Keep going and let the drawings below help guide you into your truth.

Section IV: Using The Enneagram To Enrich Your Life

Chapter 08: Integrating an ancient tool into a modern living

Having read this far, there's no denying the model of the enneagram is both simple and profoundly complex just like people.

The layers on the Enneagram system as shown in an earlier chapter then dissected into all the details you've gone through in the last two sections lead me to conclude that it would probably take a decade of deep studying to understand each of the nine types fully. Fortunately for you, it won't have to take you a decade.

In fact, all you need to get started on your self-discovery is to take a test to learn your type in the nine-point system and figure out your subtype then you can be well on your way to great revelations about your behavior, strengths and how to grow.

The good news is the more you understand why you do what you do, the easier it will become to start understanding others even if you don't necessarily know their personality type and character variation. At the very least, you will have a fresh new lens from which to interact with and understand those you encounter in your daily life. That is the power of the Enneagram of personality.

Passed on for generations from ancient times to these modern times, this system can become a handy tool for your personal growth, conflict resolution, and even character development.

Are there areas in your life you've been struggling with?

Do you have relationships that give you heartburn because you just can't seem to make them work the way you feel they should be working? Are there people in your workplace or at home you can't see eye to eye yet you know you must find a way to just get along due to the commitments held?

Is it your body that just doesn't seem to be listening to you or responding positively to anything you try?

Maybe it's the undercurrent of anger or fear or shame that you've been battling with secretly yet never quite understood.

All these issues can be improved upon with the use of this tool.

Chapter 09: Accelerating your personal growth and self-expression

Personal growth and self-expression are as essential as breathing for us as human beings. Once we secure the basic needs that help keep us feeling safe and comfortable, the longing for self-expression arises naturally. It is meant to be part of our evolution and self-realization.

Self-expression doesn't necessarily mean producing art, writing, being a performer or any of that. It can absolutely include that for certain people, but at its core, it is about communicating your truth and using body language, your work, and actions and how you interact and engage with others in your world. That also includes how you dress, the way you drive your car, decorate your home and so on.

The main challenge with personal growth and self-expression comes when there feels like there's a block or a lack of inspiration and creativity to successfully get across something that you wish to portray to another in some way.

Ever been in a situation where you really wanted to express something that was burning in your heart, but for whatever reason, you fell short of full expression which resulted in a deep sense of frustration, disappointment and this feeling that you were misunderstood?

This is a common problem when we don't yet understand ourselves and the motives, instincts, and behaviors that influence our personalities. We may have an idea of what we want to communicate, but we fall short on execution or full manifestation.

I was watching a baking show the other day, and one of the contestants who was competing to win $10,000 started crying when her cake looked nothing like what she had envisioned in her mind. Even the judges had a tough time scoring her because they could just see her anguish and the fact that she just could not make manifest whatever creative idea she had at the start of the competition.

The reason enneagram of personality tool works so well to improve people's lives is that it aids them in better understanding their strengths, hang-ups, instinctual drives and warning signs to watch out for.
But it also does something few want to talk about. This tool also brings to the foreground the underlying fears that often guide our behaviors.

Don Richard Riso and Russ Hudson reveal the nine core fears that everyone needs to become aware of in "*The Wisdom Of The Enneagram.*"

Type One: The fear of being evil or corrupt.

This personality type strives to be morally upstanding and virtuous in the face of external corruption. They tend to be perfectionists, always sweating even minute details. And their underlying fear is that they are corrupt. So the drive to be meticulous and act virtuously is driven by the need to prove that fear wrong. Motivated by their own sense of integrity, people who are type one personality will continuously strive to move away from corruption towards virtue.

Type Two: The fear of being unloved or unwanted by others

This personality type strives to be loved and wanted by those around them. They give, nurture and invest a lot of their time, effort and resources in cultivating relationships to overcome the inherent fear that they are not loveable. The giving and helping that comes from people who are in the type two personality comes from a place of proving they deserve to have care and love from others because they give it too much. They will continuously strive to move away from worthlessness and toward relationships that foster mutual loving and caregiving.

Type Three: The fear of being worthless and unaccomplished

This personality type aims to achieve success and status quo believing it to be the right measure of their own worth. The underlying fear here is an inherent feeling of worthlessness. This type feels they won't be desirable apart from their achievements and therefore must accomplish as much as possible in order to be desired and accepted by others. They will strive to continuously move aware from worthlessness and towards impressive accomplishments that can earn great admiration and respect.

Type Four: The fear of lacking a unique, special and significant identity.

With this personality type comes the need to want to prove their uniqueness and individuality to others. The underlying fear in personality type four is that he or she would be worthless and unlovable if they were "ordinary" or "average." As such, they seek to create a unique identity to prove their significance in the world.

Those who are a personality type four are continuously moving aware from normalcy and towards expressions of individuality and intensity.

Type Five: The fear of being helpless and inadequate.

This type five personality strives to be knowledgeable and competent in all he or she does. They have an underlying fear of being helpless, overwhelmed and incapable of dealing with the world around them. As a result, they attempt to learn as much as they can and master as much as they can in order to feel secure, competent and capable of handling the world. Those who are in this personality type continuously strive to move away from ignorance and ambiguity and toward knowledge and understanding.

Type Six: The fear of being without support or guidance.

This type six personality strive to find guidance and support from those around them. Their underlying fear is that they are incapable of surviving on their own. As such they are always seeking out as much support and direction from others as possible. Those who fall into this personality type continuously strive to move away from isolation and towards structure, security, and guidance of others.

Type Seven: The fear of deprivation and pain

This type seven personality strive to achieve their wildest desires and find fulfillment. Their underlying concern is that others will not meet their needs and desires. Instead, they feel they must go and pursue what they want on their own. Those in this personality type strive to move away from pain, sadness, and helplessness and towards independence, happiness, and fulfillment.

Type Eight: The fear of being harmed or controlled by others

This personality type strives to be independent, powerful, influential and self-directed. Their underlying concern is that of being betrayed, controlled or violated by others. This personality type cannot stand being controlled or at the mercy of others. They feel secure and okay only when in control of their circumstances. Those who fall into this personality type are continually moving away from external limitations toward self-sufficiency and power.

Type Nine: The fear of loss and separation from others.

This personality type strives to maintain harmony and peace both internally and externally. Their underlying fear is that they will become disconnected and separated from others. They fear they will go out of sync with the world around them. As such they will do everything possible to live in harmony with other people and the world around them because this produces that feeling of security and connectedness. Those who are in this personality type usually strive to move away from conflict and pain and toward stability, peace, and harmony.

By understanding your primary enneagram type, your basic fears, and your subtype, your natural gifts become fully appreciated, and limitations don't feel so mysterious.

It becomes easier to find satisfaction in your work and relationships. You become better equipped to deal with situations, hostile environments and your impulsive behaviors. For example, if you have a deep longing to feel needed by others, you might have issues knowing when to say "No" to something because people pleasing would be a blind spot for you. So perhaps if asked at work to do double shifts you may say, "yes" even if it hurts you. In such a situation, learning to say "No" would be the healthier more satisfying answer yet you would only have this awareness about yourself if you actually understood more about your personality type.

Some people are able to spot both their primary and subtype personalities quickly while for others it requires time, study and constant self-reflection. I don't know how long it will take you, but I encourage you to begin because the sooner you do, the quicker you'll be able to create a healthier balanced and satisfying life. Before moving on to the impact and benefit of using this tool and the insights gained to improve your relationships, I invite you to take the Enneagram test and discover your primary type as well as your wings, center, and subtype.

Chapter 10: Enneagram Test

Let's do a quick recap of the main personality types before you jump into our interactive online test:

Type one: Reformer

If this is your primary type, your focus is to make the world "right" based on your perceptions. You are purpose driven, set high standards for yourself and are very self-controlled.

Type Two: Helper

If this is your primary type, then you are driven by the need to give and take care of others. You're generous, empathic, humble and nurturing. There's a deep longing to feel loved and accepted and at times the giving can be done in an effort to secure that state of being loved.

Type Three: Achiever

If this is your primary type, then you're more focused on being the best. You want to be perceived as successful by others. You're usually very assertive, winning is everything and your personal image matters a lot.

Type Four: Romantic

If this is your primary type, then your more artistic in all you do and you have an impeccable eye for beauty. You're more attuned to your emotions and that of others and can sometimes be quite dramatic. You're a romantic at heart, and your inner fantasy world is a sanctuary to be treasured.

Type Five: Observer

If this is your primary type then your focus in on knowledge and gaining more wisdom. You're highly intellectual with a deep hunger for new ideas and greater understanding. You can articulate new paradigms in a visionary way and although you prefer solitude, when invited to speak on a topic you're passionate about you can be very welcoming and engaged.

Type six: Loyalist

If this is your core personality type, then you're full of courage. You are trustworthy and self-reliant. You often struggle with self-doubt and doubting others, which can create a rollercoaster of emotions for you, but when you're not in doubt, you're very committed and decisive.

Type seven: Enthusiast

If this is your primary type, then fun and spontaneity is your thing. You're fun, playful and pleasant to be around. You have a very positive outlook and savor the richness of the world. You tend to get easily distracted though, and you always seem to be moving to the next exciting adventure, but when not scattered around or distracted you have the potential for tremendous accomplishments.

Types eight: Challenger

If this is your primary type, then you are intense! You like to be direct with others. Productivity, high energy and excellence in your work matter to you. You're self-determined, generous and you have a big heart. Others generally perceive you as very powerful which can at times make you seem a little controlling and intimidating, especially when you're trying to gain control and influence over others.

Type nine: Peacemaker

Peace and harmony is your primary drive if you fall into a type nine personality. You are authentic, unpretentious, and patient, get along with everyone, love to serve others and put their needs first. At your best, you can recognize, encourage and help bring out the best in others.

Take the test now and once you've gotten your results to go back to section II to read a more in-depth description of your type then jump into section III to figure out what kind of a layered cake you have.

To access the test, simply copy and paste the following link into your browser:

https://bit.ly/2xEWljl

Remember we said the subtypes are like layers of a cake that we all have?

That implies you already possess all three basic instincts, but one will be more dominant. By discovering how your cake is layered, you'll start to be more awake in your daily life choices, and some of your impulses, reactions, and experiences will make more sense.

You're personality type combined with your wings and center as well as your basic instincts layered up now give you a detailed understanding of what makes you tick. And what a liberation that becomes as you step into improving your relationships with others.

Chapter 11: Cultivating Healthy Loving Relationships

Cultivating healthy, nourishing relationships is essential for all of us. But we know how tough it can be especially in our modern society with never-ending demands. That's why it's even more critical than ever before to choose your relationships wisely.

The people you associate with and invest your energy on both personally and professionally have a direct impact on your wellbeing and success. Therefore I encourage you to get better at surrounding yourself with the right people. But who would be the right person?

A critical point to remember here especially when introducing enneagram type combinations is that no paring is particularly blessed or doomed to work out. The mistake so many people make once they learn of these enneagram combinations is they avoid or undervalue all the other types. Focusing on a specific combination does not guarantee you will be happy, nourished and in love.

What you want to establish is a different objective. You want to make sure that both you and the person in question are both exhibiting the healthy versions of your types. As long as they two of you (irrespective of type) are healthy, you're experiencing together will be amazing.

Unfortunately, this isn't always the norm. That's where self-discovery and further education comes in to play. The better informed you are about the other person's type, level of health and tendencies the greater your insight going into the relationship. This is such a great tool to help you deepen your relationships, as it will make you more conscious of your behavior both positive and negative. Once you shine the light on your underlying fears, motives and natural tendencies as well as your gifts, you will have a choice about how you respond to the relationships in your life.

Regardless of your current relationship needs, whether that be building healthy professional relationships with clients or cultivating a passionate, intimate relationship with your significant other the enneagram tool can help you achieve your goals. It will help you to love more in the present and experience being more grounded in your true nature. You'll finally be in a position to recognize when you're acting out of fear and when you're acting out of your own truth. It will also enable you to discern the desires of your true self and those that are superficial.

Once you have this level of clarity and self-awareness, it becomes easy to love and live in harmony with others. Instead of reacting whenever things aren't going as you want in a relationship, you will feel empowered to respond rather than react making it possible to love, support, encourage and bring out the best in others. More importantly, you will also become a better communicator. And we all know how important communication is in a healthy relationship.

One of my best friends recently experienced the power of using this Enneagram tool to help in her self-discovery as well as her fiancé.

There is no doubt in her mind how much Tom loves her. He is the most generous, warm, appreciative, attentive, playful and nurturing man he has ever met. They make the perfect couple because he seems to compliment her personality really well. She says, " I feel so loved and special when I'm with him. There's no one else I'd want to be marrying. But he can be rather controlling, needy and insincere at times and it was really creating friction between us."

That was before I suggested they both study the Enneagram of personality test. She had already taken the test, so it wasn't too far-fetched an idea, but it took a bit of convincing before Tom agreed. In less than a month, she told me their relationship has completely transformed. She has found new ways of demonstrating her love and feels more compassion whenever some of his weaknesses show up.

They have increased their level of intimacy and communication. Above all else, their behaviors feel less like a mysterious enemy trying to sabotage their love for each other. I can only assume with time, their self-discoveries will enrich their future marriage even more.

Although I will choose to focus more on personal and more intimate relationships, the same concept can be applied to any relationship you want to work with.

Bringing back the magic of passionate love:
There's nothing more exhilarating than finding someone who "gets you." Having someone who understands you even without uttering a word is entirely magical, and I think that's a connection we all crave. When you've discovered your Enneagram type and use it to improve as well as enhance who you really are, it will then change how you approach relationships forever.

This isn't a horoscope reading but using it to figure out the best type of people who will complement and enhance your life as a whole. I'm not saying it's an exact science, but you'll be amazed at how much harmony your relationships will experience when you learn about the personality types of your loved ones. The tendencies that usually hold you back from experiencing healthy relationships with yourself and others will no longer be a mystery. After all, the happier you become, the easier it will be to nurture healthy relationships.

Suggested combination types from the Enneagram Institute.

Here are a few insights on relationships for every type that might be a great starting point if you're looking to manifest new loving relationships.

Type 1: The Perfectionist or Reformer

Best type combinations: 1 2 3 4 5 6 7 8 9

Type 2: The Giver or Helper

Best type combinations: 1 2 3 4 5 6 7 8 9

Type 3: The Achiever or Performer

Best type combinations: 1 2 3 4 5 6 7 8 9

Type 4: The Romantic or Individualist

Best type combinations: 1 2 3 4 5 6 7 8 9

Type 5: The Observer or Investigator

Best type combinations: 1 2 3 4 5 6 7 8 9

Type 6: The Loyalist or Doubter

Best type combinations: 1 2 3 4 5 6 7 8 9

Type 7: The Enthusiast or Dreamer

Best type combinations: 1 2 3 4 5 6 7 8 9

Type 8: The Challenger or Leader

Best type combinations: 1 2 3 4 5 6 7 8 9

Type 9: The Peacemaker or Diplomat

Best type combinations: 1 2 3 4 5 6 7 8 9

When it comes to finding love and cultivating relationships:

Type One: The Reformer

Having discovered this is your type and that you are motivated by the desire to live the right way, avoiding fault and blame here's your relationship suggestion.

Embrace joy and spontaneity in your relationship by proposing a spontaneous date. Yes, I know that doesn't come too easy, but with a little relaxation and the right perspective, it can be very beneficial for you. I know this is hard to hear, but the world won't crumble if you kick your heels back and relax once in a while. Release the need to control every outcome all the time. It's also wonderful to openly share with your loved ones your core values and motivations. Let them know how much you care about improving the world and invite them into that vision. Those who "get you" will be more than encouraging and supporting of your tendencies.

Type Two: The Giver

Having discovered you're warm, empathetic and motivated by the need to be needed and loved, here's your relationship suggestion.
Fight the urge to always jump in and fix other people's problems, even if you are great at it. Learn to be there for your significant other without getting too absorbed into their world and frequently step outside the box to get in touch with your feelings. Ask yourself, "How am I doing?"

Type Three: The Achiever

Having discovered, you're motivated by success, winning big and that you're wired for high performance and productivity, here's your relationship suggestion.

You have a lot to offer, not just material success and social status. Connect with that "more" that you've got. Someone's appreciation and value of you isn't always tied to your accomplishments. Learn how to make authentic connections and don't shy away from diving deep beneath the prestige and material success you have.

Type Four: The Romantic

Having discovered you're a natural romantic with an eye for beauty and more creative and expressive than most, here's your relationship suggestion.

Learn to take control of your emotions or they will control you and create constant problems within your relationships. You can become more aware of your emotions without them consuming you. Since you know, there's a tendency to be a drama queen or king and that you're particularly sensitive when feeling misunderstood, communicate this to your loved one and help them know this side of you so they too can respond accordingly when it does happen. Use your powers of perception to put yourself in the shoes of the one you love so you can see things from their side of the table, then you'll always know the right thing to do in any given situation.

Type Five: The Observer

Having discovered you're the private, analytical type motivated by a hunger to gain more knowledge, here's your relationship suggestion.

Even though you like to be detached and enjoy solitude you also know those deep, meaningful connections where there is excellent chemistry make you happy. Embrace this. Don't be afraid to be "pulled in" close by another where chemistry aligns. Your feelings aren't too much for someone else to handle, and you do have what it takes to be good at this. Learn to reconnect more with your heart so that you can know when it's the right time to make the shift from the head to the heart.

Type Six: The Loyalist

Having discovered you're the practical, committed but ever-anxious type, here's your relationship suggestion for you.

Not everyone has a "hidden agenda." I know that's hard to hear and you have a hard time being optimistic, but it won't hurt you to give people credit once in a while. Your ability to be a great and loyal friend, ever reliable and trustworthy is a power that must not be underestimated especially in our modern world. Learn to use this power to build a robust and dependable bond with a significant other.

Type seven: The Enthusiast

With the new discovery of your type as being fun, spontaneous and being motivated by pleasure seeking experiences that stimulate you, here's your relationship advice.

Your positive, fun-loving attitude is contagious and will always attract great people to you, but you must learn to push back that urge to keep fleeing away from things too quickly. Find the courage to face what might be driving you to restless and shallow activities. Being committed to the right person isn't such a bad thing you know? You have so much greatness and wisdom to offer so start working on being more centered in body and mind.

Type eight: The Challenger

There's no doubt about it, you are fierce and intense. You're powerful, full of energy, strong and motivated by a need for control and protecting the underdogs. Here's a relationship tip that can help you cultivate amazing connections.

Vulnerability especially with the one you love is not a bad thing and doesn't weaken you in their eyes. Be okay with expressing whatever emotions come up for you. People who love you can handle the real you. The real power you possess is being able to demonstrate strength as well as tenderness when the situation calls for it. Don't hold back or fight those rare moments as they will become your most magical with the one you love.

Type nine: The Peacemaker

Having discovered you're the laid back, harmonious type who always gets along with everyone here's a piece of relationship advice for you.

Yes, you are a peacemaker, but you don't always have to "settle" for something if it's not what you truly want. And being the wonderful mediator that you are, it can be easier to express your needs and desires to another even if they differ. You have permission to voice a contrasting opinion to your significant other even if it makes you uncomfortable and uneasy. The one who truly loves you will appreciate even more getting to know your frame of mind and perspective of things. So go ahead, speak your truth!

Chapter 12: Mapping out your path of most joy and fulfillment

As we said at the beginning of our journey in self-discovery and understanding the Enneagram, this typing system is based on an ancient practice that has been developed over the years to help us apply it better.

The modern Enneagram as we know it is divided into a nine-point system and subdivided into three triads or centers. The triads represent the head, the heart and the gut alternatively referred to as the thinking center, the feeling center, and the Instinctive center, which form the essential components of the human psyche.

While there are so many personality-typing systems available today, the Enneagram of personality tool stands out from the crowd and maintains its global merit for this particular reason.

It empowers you even more by offering you two pathways within your primary or dominant personality type. Not only does it dive deeper into variations you will experience even within your dominant type, but it also adds a unique aspect to things.

Namely:

You are given the direction of integration, which explains how your type is likely to behave when on a pathway of health and growth. And you're also given the direction of disintegration, which describes how your type is likely to act under pressure and stress.

This means your self-discovery goes way more in-depth than the usual personality typing systems because it gives you the power to introspect and make new conscious choices in any area of your life including relationships. It is a vital tool for anyone interested in taking their personal growth and self-awareness to the next level.

The Enneagram of personality is a tool designed to help you observe your personality (ego) and how it works more closely. Being aware of who you really are, the basic instincts that drive your behavior and the quality of character you can build to either create a healthy progressive path in life or a disintegrative one is the beginning of your self-discovery.

At a fundamental level, depending on your core personality type, there are certain passions to become vigilant of and work toward transforming. The more you reflect on your behaviors and motives the easier it will be to turn them into healthy virtues because as you recall at the start of the book, we affirmed that each of us, in essence, is pure and good.

Here is a quick recap of the passions or behaviors that may be unconsciously ruling your life plus how to transform them into healthy virtues.

Type One personality type is must work to transform his or her Anger/Resentment/Rage into Serenity.

Type Two personality type must work to transform his or her Pride into Humility.

Type Three-personality type must work to transform his or her Vanity into Integrity.

Type Four-personality type must work to transform his or her Envy into Acceptance and Equanimity.

Type Five-personality type must work to transform his or her Greed into Generosity.

Type Six-personality type must work to transform his or her Anxiety and Fear into Courage.

Type Seven-personality type must work to transform his or her Gluttony into Sobriety.

Type Eight-personality type must work to transform his or her Lust/ Intensity into Innocence/Surrender.

Type Nine personality type must work to transform his or her slothfulness/indifference into Engagement/Action.

This is why the book is laid out to help you understand what the Enneagram is and how it works before inviting you to figure out your type. The best way to figure out your type is by taking the online test that we have provided the link to in a previous chapter. By honestly answering all the questions, your top score will indicate what personality type you are. Bear in mind, you might have multiple high scores because as we said, the Enneagram is a complex, interconnected system just as a human being is complex and therefore cannot be rigidly constricted to just one strict type.

Alternatively, you could go back to the earlier chapters and read through all the detailed descriptions of all the personality types and try to decide which one is yours. If you feel like you know yourself well enough to identify your type instantly, then you may proceed on with the studying and understanding of your chosen type and all the additional information I shared in this book.

How the Enneagram can help you grow and manifest a joy-filled life.

The Enneagram is like a roadmap empowering your capacity for self-observation, and it shows you how to get to higher levels of awareness. The more you develop a clear vision of the healthiest and best version you can be, the more joyful and prosperous your life will be. It can be as simple or as complex as you desire it to be. It is recommended to start with the basics. This book covers all the basics as well as some in-depth understanding of the intricacies of the system. However, that doesn't mean our studies end there. You can still dive deeper yet into your determined core personality type, wings and subtype by venturing into what is referred to as levels of development.

In 1977 Don Riso discovered and started developing what is today known as the nine levels of development that are the internal structures that make up the personality type itself. In other words what Don Riso teaches is that you have an internal structure which constitutes the core personality you have. Within this internal structures are layers and depending on your level, a certain behavioral demonstration of your personality type will become pronounced. The range is very wide stretching from healthy, average and all the way to the lower unhealthy levels.

This discovery was further enhanced by Don Riso and Russ Hudson in the 1990s. They are the only Enneagram teachers to include this internal structure in their teachings of the Enneagram. The book recommended in chapter nine "Wisdom of The Enneagram" can also help you better understand what these teachers mean by levels of development plus how to rise higher in your development.

They developed these nine levels of development to offer a "skeletal" structure of each type, which can be very useful for therapists, counselors and other medical professions working with a client.

It can also be very useful to you when you are trying to understand another person. By learning more about the nine levels of development within their personality type and where they are along that continuum of levels at a given time, you can be able to understand whether the person is functioning within the healthy, average or unhealthy range and support them accordingly. There are other books available online by Don Riso but I specifically encourage you to check out the Wisdom of the Enneagram if you feel ready to dive into greater details of your core personality.

This isn't a requirement. You can be able to rapidly improve your work, relationships health and overall lifestyle with the information shared in this book alone. So if you're not looking to be an expert at this, fret not. You already have all the necessary knowledge to enhance your capacity for self-reflection and higher awareness. The rest will naturally unfold as you continue to work on understanding yourself and improving the areas of weakness that come to your conscious awareness.

Now that you have taken the first few steps forward, there's no going back. Your work, relationships and how you perceive yourself can never be the same again. If you've done the inner work, you'll have a better chance at controlling yourself in whatever environment or situation you end up in. You'll also have more confidence planning for your future goals. Having this inner and outer balance is what you need to thrive as your true self in our modern world. Now that you better understand and have the tool go forth and cultivate the quality of life you've always desired!

www.ingramcontent.com/pod-product-compliance
Lightning Source LLC
Chambersburg PA
CBHW031156020426
42333CB00013B/687